STRATEGIC WAYS TO THE TOP

Awesome Thoughts Everyone Must Know

For Meaningful And Successful Life

- **Religion**
- **Personality**
- **Leadership**
- **Excellence**
- **Finance**
- **Education**
- **Morality**

PRAISE FOR THE *STRATEGIC WAYS TO THE TOP*

"IN STRATEGIC WAYS TO THE TOP, the author systematically explores essential thematic topics that can strategically position every reader for his/her spot at the top. I am confident that this amazing book has something in it for every reader and that whoever reads it, imbibes it, internalizes it and applies its lessons to his/her life is working their way to the very top.

There are no limits to the heights you can attain in any facet of your life and this book is a step-by-step guide to see you through. Enjoy it and recommend it to your loved ones."

Gamel Sankarl

International Multiple Award-Winning Author
Author / Inspirational Speaker / Sensational Poet
Accra, Ghana

"Just as your best is not good enough, so also your worst is not bad enough. Complacency and despair are two dangerous thieves that rob a person of his/her desire to advance beyond their strength or limit. STRATEGIC WAYS TO THE TOP is a book that has been specifically pieced to guide you to the top. In it, you will gain the ability to master today what others will learn tomorrow. It is a MUST READ for all!!!"

David Aboagye Dacosta

Author / Inspirational Speaker / Minister of the Gospel
Jema, Ghana

"There is a spot for everyone who desires to be at the top. Edward Etse Aloryito exemplifies a young leader with a burning desire to pursue excellence. In this book, he takes us through a journey to discover what I consider the most essential wisdom nuggets when applied can get anybody to the top irrespective of career pathway or field of endeavour"

Dr. Dennis Aprese

HOD, Oral Health, College of Health and Well-Being
Kintampo, Ghana

"Do we just get to be born, grow up and start school, complete school and start work, get married and start having our own children, then subsequently die? No! There must be more to life than this. But it will take wisdom to see beyond what society has taught us to believe. And there is nothing more excellent than wisdom which is rooted in God. It is the only way we rise to the top. Because the one who guides us sits above and sees it all. Eddy's book is an important read for this generation which seems to have misplaced its priority. I am intrigued how he was able to focus on God as he explains why we MUST succeed. Brilliant!"

Capt. Dr. Paolo Rossi Adu-Gyamfi-Yeboah

Department of Surgery, Tygerberg Academic Hospital
Cape Town, South Africa

STRATEGIC WAYS TO THE TOP

Awesome Thoughts Everyone Must Know For Meaningful And Successful Life

Edward Etse Aloryito

Author / Inspirational Speaker / Medic

Unless otherwise stated, scripture quotations are from the King James and New International Versions.

Creative design by John Kyei-Fram
Typeset: Adobe Garamond Pro
Aloryito, Edward E.
ISBN 978-9988-2-4110-0

Published by Eminence Innovations
Tema, Ghana

Editing, Printing and Binding by:
Osti Media Consult and Publications
Asafo, Kumasi
Tel: (+233) 0249633154
Email: johnnyosti37@gmail.com

Request for information or enquiries should be addressed to:
Edward Etse Aloryito
Box BT 288
Tema, Ghana

Phone: (+233) 0245194693, 0202659394
Email: edwardetse@gmail.com

DEDICATIONS

To

God – Father, Son and Holy Spirit

How Awesome and Excellent are Thy Works!

And

My Twin Brother; Edmond Atsu Aloryito

&

To my Lovely Father and Dad (Mr. Emmanuel Aloryito), Everlasting Mum (Madam Helen Aglebe), Brothers (Nelson, Joshua, Raboni) and Sisters (Lucy, Esther, Regina) who have continuously sustained and inspired my dreams. You are a wonderful and amazing family. I believe God will use me to continually make you proud!

To my Mentors and Advisors: Dr. Dennis Aprese, Dr. William Okyere-Frempong, Mr Isaac Azindow, Mr David Aboagye Dacosta, Mrs Dorcas Attuah, Mr. Albert K. Batsa and Mr Gamel Sankarl. I'm grateful for your continuous guidance and support.

To my Divine Helpers: Mr. Godzo Christian, Madam Gifty Adu, Mr/Mrs Reuben Amewonya (Sey and his wife), Mary Boatemaa, John Kyei-Fram, Mr. Eric Kofi Dotse and Mr. Raymond Maalman. I'm grateful for your roles in my life.

To my Friends: All my mates, and friends. The list is too tall for me to mention names. I thank you all for your continual support.

And finally, to you the Reader!

DEDICATIONS

AKNOWLEGMENT

I am highly indebted to some contributors for their sacrifices and support in making this project a reality.

To the men who introduced me into the Leadership Arena - Dr. William Okyere-Frempong; International Leadership Expert and the CEO of The Human Development Group (HuD Group), Ghana. Mr Isaac Azindow; Former Principal, College of Health and Well-Being, Kintampo and Dr. Dennis Aprese; Dentist, Lecturer and Chaplain at College of Health and Well-Being, Kintampo. You have taught and challenged me to strategically strive for excellence. That is what has given birth to this book. God bless you.

I owe this book to the following personalities who proofread, edited the manuscript and offered excellent counsels and suggestions for improvement: Capt. Dr. Rossi Adu-Gyamfi (Medical Doctor/Army Officer), Mr Isaac Azindow; Former Principal, College of Health and Well-Being, Mr. Ebenezer O. Opoku (Lawyer/Lecturer/Business Trainer), Mr. Gamel Sankarl (Author/Poet), Mr. David Aboagye Dacosta (Author/Pastor), Mr. Stephen Apau (Lecturer), Mr. Samuel Ahiaba (Pastor/Biomedic), and Mrs. Grace Hanson (Lecturer). Your excellent counsels, criticisms, corrections, and motivations have given birth to this book. You have the strategic eyes. I am grateful to you. God bless you.

With gratitude and appreciation, I would like to acknowledge the enormous support from the Physician Assistant class (my class), other course mates, and friends who have always encouraged me. I am indeed grateful to you.

My acknowledgement would be incomplete if I fail to honour the services of John Kyei-Fram, Kofi Mensah-Amoako Junior and Osti

Media Consult and Publications. You have played tremendous roles in making this dream a reality. Thank you. May God strengthen and deepen our relationship in the coming years.

To God alone be all the glory. I thank Elohim for His grace and mercies.

TABLE OF CONTENT

FOREWORD

"Strategic Ways to the Top' is a well written work of inspiring reflections and workable strategies for anyone interested in being on top of their game. I have known the author for some time now and I can say that the thoughts he shares are not abstract but things he applies in his own life – which is headed upward. Rather than get there alone, Edward has decided to graciously share his formula for success with all of us.

It is a potent ingredient you need to include on your MUST-READ recipe for personal development. I will encourage you to pick one, read, apply the principles and let's meet at the top"

Dr. William Okyere-Frempong
The Chief Executive Officer, HuD Group, Ghana
International Leadership & Life Coach / Motivational Speaker
Accra, Ghana

PREFACE

Every great or important destination requires a number of steps to get to it. Each and every individual must accept the reality that no great achievement involves just one step. It will involve a series of steps, a series of maneuvers or a series of stratagems. Strategy is defined as a series of maneuvers that are undertaken to achieve a specific goal. Simpletons are averse to strategies. All they want is something to be done for them. If they do accept the responsibility, they do not want anything that involves more than one step.

The worst people will take zero steps to achieve anything. The worst human beings live in constant expectation of something to be done for them. Their mentality is that someone owes them something and someone has to do something for them or to them. This is often the mentality of people who have been colonized and are used to others thinking for them. Their understanding is that something has to be given to them or handed over to them. Such individuals constantly read speeches requesting aid and describing their woes, lacks and deficiencies and hoping that this will touch the heart of a philanthropist somewhere. Even after many years they do not perceive that their woeful plight and pathetic situation does not touch the hearts of many people in this selfish world. It takes years for zero-step people to realize that no one will freely pour out his hard-earned wealth into their laps.

Who are we and what at all is expected of us? It is prudent we allude to our earthly manual so we better understand and appreciate our true nature and being. God wants us, the people He made in His image and likeness, to become like Him in character and industry. God expects nothing but the best from His children. When we excel, He smiles, but

He becomes sad when we exhibit mediocrity. Whoever excels is by that reflecting the Character and the Image of God.

God is a God of Excellence in Character. Throughout the book of Psalms, there is a vivid description of how Excellent God is. The Psalmist mused, "O LORD Our Lord, how excellent is thy name in all the earth! Who has set thy glory above the heavens", Psalm 8:1. Again, the Psalmist makes a passionate request, "Let them praise the name of the LORD: for His name alone is excellent; His glory is above the earth and heavens", Psalm 148:13. The name and character of God are excellent. Because He is Excellent in character, He has warned us not to mention His name in vain. God's name cannot be treated with disdain. God is excellent in relationship. Another way by which God demonstrates His Excellency is through His relationship with humankind. God's mercies, kindness and His treatment of us cannot be fathomed. Our sins qualify us for outright rejection and death penalty, yet He treats us as though we have not sinned, an exhibition of His excellent relationship with us. He daily provides us with food, air, water, shelter, security, peace, et cetera. He treats us the way He would want us to treat Him. God is awesome.

God is Excellent in power and greatness. Who can be compared to our God in power and might? Imagine the world hanging in space without anything keeping it on hold! Imagine the distance from the earth to the sun – precision at its best. Look at the sky, the seas, and the fountains of the water and ask: Who made all these things? God! God is Excellent in creation. The repetitive statement in the first three chapters of the book of Genesis confirms this, "And God saw that it was good". Another interpretation of this is that, "And God saw that all what He had created was Excellent" Prophet Isaiah after several contemplations, burst out, "Sing unto the LORD; for He hath done excellent things: this is known in all the earth," Isaiah 12:5.

Since God, the creator, owner, sustainer of life and the world is excellent in all His ways and dealings, it is imperative and a divine obligation and heavenly mandate for all who were created in His image and likeness to strive for excellence in all our ways. In everything we do as people who believe in Him, excellence must be the watchword; anything less is a denial of faith. We cannot be God's children and live a mediocre lifestyle. God is not a mediocre God.

To become excellent in any field of endeavour, you need to adopt and master series of steps and strategies. You need excellence to reach the top. Excellence brings you success, wealth, fame, influence, respect and regard, peace of mind, happiness, et cetera. To get to the top, you must possess the strategic skills. It is impossible to influence your generation and the world at large and enjoy all the earlier mentioned benefits if you are not strategic. My questions are: Have you reached the top where you so much desired to be? Are you satisfied and happy with where you are now? Have you attained excellence in your field of endeavour? Are you strategic? Have you identified all that you need to attain excellence? What influence and regard do you command? Are your services in demand? How do your thoughts become results? What pace have you set for others to follow? Have you identified **ALL** your talents, gifts and skills and fully exploited them? If you can't answer all these questions in the affirmative, then you are holding the right book in your hand.

Reaching the top is not about having a degree with first class honours or attaining the highest academic qualification. What then do you need? **STRATEGIC WAYS TO THE TOP** has uncovered and answered almost all questions begging for answer in living meaningful, impactful and excellent life. The book systematically shows the way to the top and how you should climb the strategic ladder to the top. I am confident that as you read through this book word by word, sentence by sentence, paragraph by paragraph, page by page, chapter by chapter, you will discover the gem and the secrets for excellently reaching your peak.

Here is a poem for your reading pleasure. This is written by one of African's finest poet, Gamel Sankarl.

TO THE TOPMOST TOP

We're going to the very top
We're never going to stop
We've seen in our vision pot
We have at the top, our spot
We've been granted grace
We're going to win the race
This is our hope; our promise
And we'll never compromise
This is our life's call; our charge
And we'll keep to it and be large
We will dance to the beat
No matter how hot the heat
We will do our very best
We will not relax or rest
We will not slack or be lazy
We will work like we're crazy
We are presently right here
But we will surely get there
We're going to the very top
We'll never renege or stop

GOD'S APPENDED SIGNATURE AND APPROVAL

Genesis 1:27-28 reads "So God ***created man in his own image***, in the image of God he created him; male and female he created them. God blessed them and said to them, '***Be fruitful and increase in number;*** fill the earth and ***subdue it. Rule over*** the fish of the sea and the birds of the air and over every living creature that moves on the ground'. Then God said, "***I give you every seed-bearing plant on the face of the whole earth and every tree that has fruit with seed in it. They will be yours for food***"

Jeremiah 1:5 says "***Before I formed you in the womb I knew you, before you were born I set you apart;*** I appointed you as a prophet to the nations"

Jeremiah 29:11 reiterates "For ***I know the plans I have for you***, declares the LORD, 'plans to ***prosper you*** and not to harm you, plans to ***give you hope and a future."***

Matthew 7:11 noted that "If you, then, though you are evil, know how to give good gifts to your children, ***how much more will your Father in heaven*** give good gifts to those who ask him!"

John 3:16 confirms that "For God so love the world that he gave his only begotten Son, that ***whoever believes*** in him shall not perish but have eternal life."

The above five scriptural references (and many others) have confirmed that we all have one Heavenly Father who is so much concerned about our welfare and how we live our lives here on earth. He wants nothing but the **BEST** for us. But in the last scripture quoted above (John 3:16), our Father has given us the choice to make individual decisions on our own. This is evident by the phrase "***whoever believes***" in the verse. God has demonstrated pure democratic principles here. For your information, democracy started since time immemorial (since creation commenced). This implies that to live an excellent Godly and meaningful life is entirely our choice. God has no role to play in that decision. Remember God has appended His signature and approved you as His son or daughter but you must take the conscious decision to wake up and remain in that reality.

There are immeasurable and countless number of lessons we must learn from the works of God. One of such lessons is how strategically and systematically He created the universe. God used six days in creating the universe. My question is: why didn't God create everything altogether the same day but He created some before others? He could have created all things within a day because it was not too difficult for Him but He failed to do that.

Why? It is because He wanted to teach us great lessons from the creation story. He wanted to teach us the real importance of taking one step at a time even though there are many steps needed to be taken to reach the intended and divine destination in life. That is why He created the world in the way He created it. Again, the creation story also reminds us of the fact that only one or two or three step(s) is/are not enough to guarantee us a safe arrival at our peak in life. You must continuously adopt and apply several steps that will benefit you on your way to divine fulfillment. Steps are strategies. After employing several steps in creating this amazing universe in a systematic manner, Bible records that He rested on the seventh day because everything that He made now appeared "Excellent". If God used systematic approach and strategies in creating the world and at the end of His work, His work was excellent, then we as His children have no excuse not to adopt and employ the relevant strategies in life. Because at the peak of life, we are likely to see our life as "Excellent" as our Father saw His handiwork.

Once again, after Adam fell, God had a perfect plan in redeeming and reconciling man unto Himself but this didn't happen overnight. God had to use well-articulated, calculated and orchestrated strategies and steps in redeeming man. He had to systematically and carefully choose a genealogy from which the Messiah would come and save humanity. God used so many years to achieve this by working through servants He chose to use in accomplishing the task. God chose and worked through the Abrahamic genealogy. Let's see how it happened, ***"Thus there were fourteen (14) generations in all from Abraham to David, fourteen (14) from David to the exile in Babylon, and fourteen (14) from the exile to the Messiah", Matthew 1:17.*** It took God **forty-two (42)** different generations in order to accomplish the thought of redeeming and reconciling man unto Himself. What a strategic God!!! He has again confirmed the use of **strategies** in achieving the **best** result. If He had used anyone from any of the generations, His original intent would not have been fulfilled and the best result would also not have been achieved. It's a lesson we must learn.

God demands only the best, nothing less. God is displeased with a lifestyle of mediocrity, substandard products and services. He is a God of excellence and therefore does not associate Himself with anything that is rubbed in mediocrity. All His created works are excellent. He always goes for the Best for Himself and always gives nothing short of the Best for His children.

For instance, when Adam fell, God gave us Jesus – one of heaven's best gifts. After Christ ascended, He gave us another excellent gift, the Holy Spirit. When it comes to the construction of the Tabernacle in the wilderness, God chose the best Artisans and materials to build it. Every detail of the plan of the Tabernacle was given to the Artisans through Moses so that the Artisans do not use their own plans to construct the building. When the Tabernacle was completed and ready, God again chose the best among the children of Israel to work in the temple as priests and ministers. As if that was not enough, when it came to which types of animals to be used for sacrifices to Him, God did not only choose the cleanest animals, but also warned the people against offering unto Him defective animals. You remember Cain and Abel story? It was therefore not amazing that He became angry at His people for offering defective animals to Him after the Babylonian captivity, (Malachi 1:6-8). With regard to farm produce, only the best of the first fruits from the people's farms was to be brought to the temple. King Solomon, Abel, King David knew this secret. King Solomon knew His God so well that when he was also putting up a temple for God, He did it excellently.

It is "Divine Treason and Error" to lower the excellent standard God has set for Himself. God accepts neither 90% nor 99.9% of commitment to

Him, but only a hundred percent commitment from anyone who would want to relate to Him. That is why only the Best will make it to heaven. Only the Best is good enough for the Lord. Since God demands only the best for Himself and for us, we must not settle for anything less than the best whether we are Christians or not. It is a denial of faith for a Christian to lower God's standard of Excellence.

With full consciousness that God has appended His signature and approved of your dreams and ambitions, take a decision to break bounds and pursue excellence.

BREAK BOUNDS AND PURSUE EXCELLENCE

"When you strive to successfully break bounds and pursue excellence in your chosen field with an unshakable enthusiasm and a very strong desire, you become the standard with which others are measured" Edward Etse Aloryito

A time is coming and that time is now when only multitalented people and bounds breakers will matter most in the world. Our world systems coupled with daily technological advancement are moving at a very high velocity such that you will be left behind and lost in life's wilderness forever if you don't pursue excellence. We are all matter but if you want to matter, you must break bounds with excellence. Even though it is not everyone who can matter, you must choose to matter by having insatiable and inseparable affinity for excellence. Strive to be a yardstick of quality.

In life, there are so many people who are sitting at their place of endeavor. There are others who are standing in their fields of endeavor. Only few people are standing out. If you really want to make a recognizable impact, fulfill your destiny, live meaningfully and joyous, influence your generation and leave an undeletable legacy, you have to stand out. To stand out is to be of quality and value. It is not just enough to be standing. You can only be seen when you stand out of the crowd. People have set records and made history for themselves simply because they dared to break bounds and pursued excellence with all their intrinsic energy and abilities. These people are different from you but are not better than you. You were all created by the same God. You have the same spiritual wiring in your neurological system and genes. The truth is that you have not challenged yourself to break the bounds created by others. Your success is blocked by someone's standard he set some years ago. Who told you, you can't break that record and set a new one?

"If, after all, men cannot always make history have a meaning, they can always act so that their own lives have one" Albert Camus

This is the secret. To break bounds and make history in your family, dare to do things your parents and family members feared most to do. To leave a legacy in your locality, profession or place of work, dare to exceptionally do what no one has been able to do in that locality or profession or work place. Set the pace for others to follow. You have what it takes to set the pace. Endure all the pain that comes with daring to be different. Move one step at a time. Small step is enough to make you start. Focus on the crown and the glory that comes at the end of the battle. Let that motivate and propel you in the storm.

In the book, *Believe You Can* (p.72), John Mason (Author) told a story that has made me restless ever since I read the book four years back. The story has been paraphrased in the three paragraphs below.

In the latter part of the nineteenth century, when the Methodist Church was holding its denominational convention, one leader stood up and shared his vision both for the church and the society at large. He told the ministers and the evangelists how he believed someday men would fly from place to place instead of merely travelling on horseback. It was a concept too difficult and impossible or outlandish for many members of his audience to handle.

One minister, Bishop Wright, stood up and angrily protested. "Heresy!" he shouted. "Flight is reserved for the angels!" He went on to elaborate that if God had intended for man to fly, He would have given him wings. Clearly, the Bishop was unable to envision what the speaker was predicting. When Bishop Wright finished his brief protest, he gathered up his two sons, Orville and Wilbur, and left the auditorium.

Several years later, on December 17, 1903, those two sons did what their father publicly objected to and called impossible: they recorded the first human flight (four times). They simply decided to break bounds created by their father. Yesterday ended last night. So today is more valuable to look ahead and prepare than to look back and regret. John Barrymore observed, "A man is not old until regrets take the place of dreams" Five years on, you will regret things you didn't do now than the things you did.

Why do Africans continue to celebrate Dr. Kwame Nkrumah and Nelson Mandela? They dared to lead their subjects differently. Twenty seven years of imprisonment could not tame Nelson Mandela to bring him under submission. They broke the chains of mediocrity and pursued excellence. Just like Bishop Wright, many colleagues of Dr. Kwame Nkrumah and Nelson Mandela could not fathom and comprehend the visions of these great leaders because their visions transcend the imaginations of their audience. Why do we respect and celebrate Kofi Annan? Your guess is as good as mine.

There are so many journalists in Ghana but why do we keep hailing Anas Aremeyaw Anas? He dared to skillfully do what journalists feared to do. He added a new value and dimension to Ghanaian journalism. He has set the pace. There are so many international journalists who have passed on to eternity but why do we keep celebrating Komla Dumour? He dared to be different. Because he dared to be different, he left an indelible mark. So many boxers have died but why was the entire world mourning the death of Mohammed Ali? He dared, challenged and beat George Foreman, the then world heavy weight champion at age 22 at the time no one expected it. He changed the face of boxing by bringing poetry into it. He is the boxer with the highest philosophical quotes.

There are countless number of computer programmers in the world but why is Mark Zuckerberg on the lips of many? He decided to set a different pace for the world to follow. At age 31, Mark Zuckerberg is richer than Ghana as a nation plus the wealth of all Ghanaians combined. What about Bill Gates, Oprah Winfrey, Steve Jobs, and Warren Buffet? What have they done differently from others to have gotten the recognition and the wealth they have? I'm sure you now know their secret. Footballers and coaches are many and almost everywhere but it appears as if by default when sports pundits and lovers (enthusiasts) open their mouth, they are likely to mention names like Lionel Messi, Christiano Ronaldo, Neyman, Zidane, Mourinho, Alex Fergusson, Pep Guardiola and the like. What has Usain Bolt done differently from other sprinters? They all have a secret and you know it now – They broke bounds and pursued excellence.

Pastor Dr. Mensa Otabil, Rev. Eastwood Anaba, Rev. Sam Korankye Ankrah and Bishop Dag Heward Mills are Ghanaian gospel preachers who do not own television channels or radio stations yet most Christians home and abroad still make time and watch and listen to their television programs because of their wisdom and their impact. These personalities have made more impact than most television channel and radio station owners. They have a secret and the secret is they have broken the bounds and pursued excellence. What has Sarkodie done differently in his secular music career? What has Sonnie Badu done that has somewhat shot him ahead of his peers in the gospel industry? What about Kwame Despite, what has he done differently among his colleague entrepreneurs? What has Aliko Dangote done to get to his current status?

In our educational institutions, there are different grades obtained by different students in the same class who have all been taught by the same teacher. These grades have remarks attached to them. There is a reason for these remarks. It ranges from excellence, very good, good, average, weak and very weak. These are remarks that show our academic strength or weakness in a particular subject or course or sometimes in a general exam after results from all subjects have been compiled and computed. Nobody goes into an examination room with the mindset to fail. Most often than not, our preparedness before the exams reflects the remarks we will obtain after the exams.

Always prepare for the "excellent" remark. Don't settle for anything less. "Excellent" means you have obtained 80 marks or above. 100% is achievable in exams. 100% is achievable in your field of calling or profession. You know why? – If it is not achievable, it wouldn't have been part of the marks or measurement. Excellence can only be achieved by people who have purposed it in their hearts to break bounds.

A time is coming and that time is now when only multitalented people and bounds breakers will matter most in the world. We are all matter but if you want to matter, break bounds with excellence. Even though it is not everyone who can matter, you must choose to matter by having insatiable and inseparable affinity for excellence.

WHY THERE SHOULD BE A CASE FOR EXCELLENCE

It is not just a word; it is an attitude, a mindset, a lifestyle. Excellence simply means: To go beyond the ordinary, to surpass in good quality. It is also used in contexts to mean something that is: Notable, Eminently good, Premium, Exceptional, Distinction, Topnotch, First class, High grade, of the very best kind, et cetera. The enemies of this lifestyle include: Ordinary, Inferior, Substandard, Second class, Mediocre, among others.

Booker T. Washington shows the way to achieve it: "To do a common thing in an uncommon way". According to Raph Marston, "It is not a skill but an attitude". The famous Greek Sage, Aristotle, puts it this way: "It is an art won by training and habituation. Excellence is therefore not an act but a habit". And clearly habits can be developed or acquired.

To achieve the attitude of excellence, the Father of American Education has advised, "Excellence is never an accident; it is the results of high intention, sincere efforts, intelligent direction, skillful execution and the vision to see obstacles as opportunities". In other words, someone who aspires for excellence must be prepared and willing to: Risk more than others think it is safe, love more than others think it is wise, dream more than others think it is practical, go the extra mile more than others think is normal and expect more than others think is possible. "Champions do not become champions when they win the event (or the award). The championship is in the hours, weeks, months and years, they spend preparing for it. The victorious performance itself is merely the demonstration of their championship character", Alan T. Armstrong has observed. Studies have shown that the best way to achieve excellence in fields such as sport, music and scholarship is through practice – constant practice. Achievement of excellence in such fields, according to the study, is approximately 10 years of dedication, comprising about 10,000 hours of effort.

When it comes to leaders – President, CEO, Manager, Pastor, Doctor, Lawyer, et cetera, why do nations and corporate organizations always opt for the best to lead or manage affairs? Why do they not choose the ordinary person? Why are people willing to pay huge sums of money to listen to a particular speaker and yet when it comes to others, they would not even ask how much the ticket is selling? Why would you sleep in an excellent hotel rather than a good one?

Why did Jesus attract more followers in His days on earth than the rest of the teachers of the Law and the Pharisees who were on the ground even before Christ started his ministry? Mediocrity is not the reason. Excellence rather is the contributing factor. Quality attracts quantity. Excellent performance in any field of endeavour attracts quantity. Excellent products and services have the magnetic force to attract high patronage. It is therefore not surprising that Jesus attracted more followers than the Pharisees. Excellence is the reason some movies, books, music, products and services get huge patronage when others do not. Here are benefits derived from excellence in any endeavour.

EVERY SOCIETY AND ORGANIZATION LOVES EXCELLENCE

It is morally unacceptable for any citizen not to do his or her best in any field of calling. Every nation, society, corporate organizations, and religion demands excellence from its people. Over the years, excellence has been and will continue to be one of the major symbol or icon or identifying marks of organizations and institutions. Perhaps you have often heard it said by corporate entities: "Excellence our motto"; "Excellence is our hallmark"; "Excellence awards"; et cetera. Even the motto of Eminence Analytic and Research Institute, Ghana (EARIG, thus my institute) is "Professionalism and Excellence". The people I associate myself with are people who have excellence as their aim. Every corporate entity expects nothing but excellent performance from her employees. Not so many months ago, ten percent of the employees of a corporate organization were sacked for non-performance. Excellence is an automatic expectation of every society and organization, and failure to meet set standard has severe consequences; you might not enjoy your life as you should. Your certificate or links may get you a job, but it takes excellence to maintain and keep you there. If you want to stand out from the crowd, you must strive for excellence because that is the only way out.

EXCELLENCE IS AN ASSET

Why are some people's services in higher demand than others? Why are some products in higher demand than others? Why are some computer brands, cars, mobile phones, electronic gadgets, clothing, et cetera in higher demand than others? Why do some preachers, teachers, motivational speakers have their dairies full of appointments and invitations when their contemporaries have almost theirs empty? Recently, I was part of a delegation that went to a renowned preacher for booking and appointment for a programme which is one year ahead of time. Yet we could not succeed because he was booked two years ahead of time. His schedule for the next two years was full. One word explains why: Excellence. When you excel, people will be in demand of you. When you excel, the world will listen to you, and you will become a symbol and an icon to many people. When you excel, people and companies will fight over your time. When you excel, you dictate how things should be done and people will listen and take your instructions and act on it. When you excel in your field, you get what you want in life.

Who are the ones who get sponsored for further studies from a graduating class of a university? The answer is clear – the First Class Graduates and also Topnotch Lecturers. In corporate organizations, it is always the best, in fact, the very best of the employees who get sponsored to attend international seminars, refresher courses or go for further studies. They are the ones who are promoted very early, receive increase in remunerations, get fat salaries, et cetera. The reason is obvious and predictable: outstanding attitudes resulting in excellent performance; it is an asset. Let no one deceive you. If you want to be famous, powerful, rich, influential, recognized, regarded and respected, get an asset called Excellence. An excellent woman – a woman with character and beauty will make the best home and will have no problem in marriage. Men and women fight over such ones. They dictate who they want. Strive to become excellent in whatever you do, for it is an asset.

EXCELLENCE SUSTAINS YOUR JOB

The better a person is at doing his work; the less likely it is that he or she will be replaced. In simple terms, if it is difficult to find someone exactly like you to do what you are good at doing, it shows that you excel in your field. There are some workers like that in various offices, who would be extremely difficult to replace. These people have job security. When there is shaking up at the work place, they are not affected. Why would any football club in the world be willing to pay Lionel Messi, Christiano Ronaldo, Neyman, Suarez and the like huge sums of money for the services of these players? It is because when you excel in your chosen field, your job is secured. Not only is your job secured, you also get what you want. Excellence provides job security; it protects those who have it. It saves life.

Ponder over this scenario that occurred in a corporate organization recently. One morning, when all the workers arrived for work, they were called to an emergency meeting. The agenda was simple: Due to poor economic indicators, as well as the rising cost of production, management has agreed that 20% of its labour force was to be declared redundant. Which category of the workers do you think are likely to stay on and which are likely to go? The answer is predictable – the best among them stayed because no sensible CEO or MD of a company would want to lose his best employees. In both the corporate and private worlds, a person who excels in his or her field is more likely to receive help and support in times of crisis than the one who is average or good. There are places some people can go to where others cannot. There are doors that will open to some people but not to others. Proverb answers: *"Do you see a man who excels in his work? He will stand before kings; He will not stand before unknown men" Proverbs 22:29*

EXCELLENCE DRAWS ATTENTION

Nothing short of the best satisfies the tastes, desires and wants of mankind. This explains why people prefer quality products to inferior ones. Granted you have the means to watch any of the following matches, which one will you watch – a football match between Chelsea and Manchester United or one between Sunderland and a Premier Championship (First Division) Club? Imagine you have the means to buy any of the following, which one will you buy – a brand new car or a used car, a store laptop or a used one, a fresh bread or a two day old bread? Granted you can afford the tuition fee of any of the universities in the world, which one will you opt for? Given the chance to choose between attending a seminar by David Oyedepo and one by a less known personality (both motivational speakers), which one will you attend?

The answers to the above questions are obvious. Because excellence is appealing, as compared to mediocrity, the excellent ones in the above scenario will attract you more than the mediocre ones. The desire for the best is part of our make-up. That is how God created us. In a corporate recruitment exercise, a person with excellent CV, attitude, dressing, is likely to be hired over someone with less impressive outlook and records.

Even in most university admissions, people with excellent grades and results are more likely to be admitted than those with good or low grades. Craving for the best is embedded in our very nature; that is why excellent things attract us over mediocre ones.

PEOPLE ADMIRE, HONOUR AND REWARD EXCELLENCE

What happened in Ghana (specifically) and the world at large when President Professor John Evans Atta Mills died? What happened throughout Africa and the rest of the world when Komla Dumour died? What happened in the United States, the boxing fraternity and the world over when Mohammed Ali died? What happened in the entire world when Myles Munroe died in a plane crash? In all these cases, the entire world mourned those personalities. World leaders, Business moguls, Shakers and Movers of the world economy, International Stars, etc. abandoned their daily schedules, and attended the funerals of those eagles. Why? Because they were icons of excellence.

Nowhere in the world would people organize or attend an award ceremony to reward people for mediocre achievement. No, it will never happen. On the contrary, you might have heard about or attended an Excellence Award. Why do you think mediocrity is not awarded? Why are some people favoured above others even though they may all be of the same age, or have the same qualification and experience? Regardless of favouritism and corruption, the truth remains that excellent people are preferred over average ones in any endeavour. It is for the same reason that some would listen to a particular radio station and not others; watch particular television stations and not watch others.

I am of the fullest conviction that people like Kwame Sefa-Kayi (Peace FM), Abeiku Santana (Okay FM), Bernard Avle, Richard Dela Sky, Jessica (all Citi FM), Aku Mama Zimbi (Adom FM), Kwesi Pratt Jnr. (TV3), and some other journalists will get job tomorrow if their employers make mistake and fire them today; others may have to stay home for months and perhaps years. I was not shocked at all when Nana Aba Anamoah immediately got another job after the controversial incident that led to her dismissal at TV3 in the latter part of last year (2015). Excellence has a reward! Period. People respect and reward Excellence. Excellence makes all the difference. Our world honours, rewards and respects people of excellence. As a result, they are in high demand.

People who excel cannot escape popularity. But not all popular people excel. Note the difference. When you excel in your field of endeavour, no matter where you come from, your level of education, colour, religion, gender or creed, people will recognize, respect and reward you. It is excellence that has caused Boutros Boutros-Ghali and Kofi Annan (Africans) to become the United Nations Secretary General. When you excel in your work, nobody can say NO to you and your requests. Perhaps you know better than I do, the United Nations will not choose just any person to be its Head – they go for only the best.

Excellence is the reason some African countries pay so much money to foreign coaches to handle and manage their national football teams. Excellence is the reason some presidents and governments in certain countries are performing better than their colleague presidents (with their governments inclusive) in other countries. If you want to be respected, counted, have a pay rise, be promoted, there is only one way: Strive for Excellence. That is the way to the top.

In summary, in whatever field of endeavour you find yourself, remember that the quality of your life: promotions, salary increment, et cetera will be directly proportional to your commitment to excellence. The excellent way to make money in this life is not to chase it, but excel in whatever you do. If you are the best in your field, money, fame, promotion, quality of life and peace of mind will chase you. When you excel, things pursue you, you do not pursue them. Confucius sums up this way, "The will to win, the desire to succeed, the urge to reach your full potential...these are the keys that will unlock the door to personal excellence". In order to overcome average personality or performance, make it your aim every day to settle for nothing below excellence. Decide that whatever you do or touch shall bear the hall-mark of excellence. In the words of the late Steve Jobs (Apple genius), "Be a yardstick of quality". It is not surprising that Apple products are yardstick of quality. The next time you see or buy an apple IPhone, Ipad, Imac, et cetera, you are holding in your hands a quality product that came from a man who made excellency his yardstick.

You can't break bounds and pursue excellence, unless you have successfully identified your talents and passions and develop them well. How do you do that? The next chapter takes you through it.

1. Anthony Melchizedeck O. (2014), *The Eagle's Mindset,* ISBN 978-9-9881-9048-4

IDENTIFY YOUR TALENTS AND PASSIONS

"An ambition is what you aspire to achieve and an assignment is what God desires that you accomplish. When an ambition aligns with a God-given assignment, attainment becomes inevitable" -Gamel Sankarl

Talent is a natural aptitude or skill. Talent can also be a special ability that allows someone to do something well. If you are very good at something, you have a talent. Passion on the other hand, is a strong and barely uncontrollable emotion. When passion aligns with talent, the sky is not even your limit. No one has only one talent. We individually have a mixture of talents. The problem is that many people focus on identifying, nurturing and developing only one talent or gift or skill leaving the rest to lie dormant and unproductive in them. The day you start identifying and developing the mixture of talents in you, the people around you and the entire world will stand in awe at your multiple manifestations.

A time is coming and that time is now when only multitalented people will matter most in the world. Wake up to the reality and identify, grow and groom your multiple talents before time catches up with you.

WHAT MOVES AND DRIVES YOU?

There is a driving force that drives everyone towards his/her talent. It is so irresistible that no external power or influence can over shadow it. It has a very loud voice which commands from within your inmost being and makes you restless. It cannot be tamed, suppressed or subdued. It is a voice which needs prompt obedience for action. Anytime, an occasion of your talent is organized, even with late notice, before you could realize, you are already at the venue. You can't just control yourself.

What makes you irresistible? What activity drives you? What makes you willingly miss your favourite meal or other home meals? Which profession drives you? Is it the drive to become a well respectable and renowned doctor, lawyer, business man, teacher, administrator, pastor, politician, journalist, sportsman, farmer, military man/woman, musician, et cetera? Find it out. You are the best person to know it for yourself. As a child, what moved David most was his passion to lead his sheep to feed on the pasture. No wonder he became a great leader because he started leading at a tender age. (1st Samuel 17:34)

WHAT KEEPS YOU AWAKE?

"On my bed I remember you; I think of you through the watches of the night" Psalm 63:6

There are several and countless times when you all of a sudden wake up from a deep sleep in the middle of the night and you can no longer sleep again. Not that you aren't willing to sleep again, but just that a particular giant thought, imagination and meditation has completely stolen your sleep away from you. It starts like a rain droplet and progressively but slowly moves from just being a thought and gradually translates into your superconscious mind with strong and uncontrollable emotion such that you lay very quiet on the bed with your eyes open.

The next thing you start seeing is that you see yourself in many images in your mind's eye performing exactly what you are thinking about. This mental imagery continues for an appreciable number of minutes and even hours before it finally closes in the manner it started.

Note this. That particular thought came not just for the fun of it. It came because it needed to be attended to. That is why it came in the most precious moment and time of your life. It came at the time when there is probably no body awake to disturb your attention and concentration. Most of the time, it is actually that thought that came to wake you up. It requires your maximum attention. It is God who has brought you that thought.

Write it down and start acting on it. This is how your talents and passions communicate with you. They come to you deep into the night for that communication. If you accept them, they will stay with you and multiply your life in thousand folds that will benefit you and your generation and even generations yet unborn. If you reject the thought, you have rejected your talent and passion; they will be with you but lay dormant and unproductive. What keeps you awake? Find it out. You are the only one to remember the kind of conversations you have had with your talents and passions any time they visit you.

Again, in the verse quoted above, David made us to understand that there was something that was keeping him awake. When David got closer to and knew what was making him have sleepless nights, he found comfort, joy, peace of mind and pleasure.

WHAT MAKES YOU HAPPY?

"I was glad when they said unto me 'Let us go into the house of the Lord'" Psalm 122:1

It is not every activity or engagement that makes us happy. There are some activities that you have performed which you wouldn't have done if you had the chance. It is because you don't like and love them, that is why you don't feel happy performing them. There are the others too that make you so happy any time you perform them. Even if you are suppressed by your parents or by whatever circumstances, you still at the least opportunity end up performing that very activity you were warned never to engage in. They make you feel some fulfilment and a sense of joy.

All boil down to passion and enthusiasm with which you perform these activities. When you succeed in knowing your talents and passions, any activity related to them makes you happy and fulfilled. Performance in such endeavours gladdens your spirit man. What activity or profession gives you happiness in your inmost being any time you are performing it or even just at the mention of it?

David was happy going to the house of the Lord because that is the place where he demonstrated most of his music/singing and instruments playing talents and skills respectively. Even as a King, he was playing instruments and singing hymns because that was what made him happy. It was this talent that saved him from the plots of his immediate predecessor Saul in the latter's house. Sometimes God can make it possible for your talent to deliver you from troubles.

WHAT DO YOU DO WITHOUT STRUGGLE?

People struggle in doing what they were not divinely called to do. If you have a divine calling in that which you do or you wish to do, you will not struggle. There are activities or tasks you can use one week to perform with or without preparation, yet others can use approximately one month to do that same thing even after they have gone through massive preparation. It is never pathetic or surprising at all. It just confirms God's power and the different kinds of gifts and talents we individually possess.

The world economy, governance, education, religious front, arts, journalism, et cetera are under perpetual struggle and failing today because majority of the people who are not divinely called to lead are those at the helm of affairs. Money and corruption has made it possible for square pegs to be put into round holes. How can they fit? The sad and funny revelation is that the occupants of such positions know they don't qualify and deserve where they are. They aren't happy and very frustrated in life. Never allow money and corruptions determine your dwelling and status in life.

If you struggle in doing anything, humbly quit it and focus on the ones you do with no struggle. I am not a singer so I would never venture into music. I am not a footballer so I will never venture into it as a career. I can only support someone with that divine calling with prayers or my finances. What do you do without struggle? Ponder over it. Stop chasing the things you struggle to do whilst you leave those you can do with ease.

Stop chasing someone's niche. Search for your own niche and occupy it because it is only in your niche that you can better yourself. That is the only place you can divinely and fully influence the world from and accomplish that which you were ordained to do.

One of the things David never struggled to do is that he never struggled to win on a battle field. He started killing lions at a tender age so to him, fighting and killing Goliath was just one of the many life-threatening battles he won earlier in life. He is known in the Bible as a warrior because of the many battles he fought and won as a child and as a King. He knew all the strategic plans to adopt in a battle field in order to be victorious. (1st Samuel 17:34-37)

WHAT CAN YOU DO BEST OR DO YOU DO BEST?

Anything you don't struggle in doing, you can do it best if you are dedicated and committed to doing it. There are some things you can do best with small preparation or rehearsal. It is naturally with you so it needs only one or two rehearsal to perfect it. There are others that you can only do best with very consistent and unwavering self-discipline and training.

You have more than one talent. You have multiple talents. The fact is that you don't know you have those talents. Identified talents give you passions. There are so many things you do best or you can do best. But the problem is that you haven't sat down for a moment to ponder and brood over it. This is the moment to ask you this question.

What can you do best or do you do best? Is it singing, decoration, teaching, debating, public speaking, preaching, writing, leadership, drumming, organizing, sporting activities, et cetera? Identify your talents and develop them because that is where your wealth is. If you can be true to yourself, you have a mixture of talents in you. For instance, if you are a debater, you can be a public speaker as well. If you are a singer, you can preach as well with your music. What do you do best or can you do best? I believe we all know what David could do best.

HOW DO YOU FEEL WHEN PEOPLE SHODDILY DO WHAT YOU DO BEST?

There have been many circumstances and instances where I strongly felt I should assume leadership role and take charge as I saw leaders (with students' leadership inclusive) performing abysmally in least expected events and leadership mantles. I am very certain I'm not the only person who has ever felt like that before. You have also done same before in your field of calling as you saw someone messing up in what you do best. It is a natural feeling and that is also a confirmation and an indication of your talent. This explains why David got angry when Goliath was threatening the Israelites and defying their God. (1st Samuel 17:26)

HOW TO DEVELOP YOUR TALENTS AND PASSIONS

After genuinely answering the six important questions above, you would be in a better position to know your talents and passions with clarity. After knowing your talents with precision and conviction, you must develop them into ambition. Let your talent and passion become your ambition in life. This can only see the light of the day if you commit it in prayer to God. Talents come easily but usually they are raw. For it to get to the point where it is sought after, one must develop it. David had a talent in music. But he constantly played the harp anytime he got the opportunity. Have you realized that it was the harp that took him to Saul's palace? You are bound to losing your talents if you fail to develop them. David would have lost his if he had not continuously developed them.

Identify your talent, passion and ambition and let that be your driving force for excellence. You need formal, informal and all other forms of education to grow and develop your talents. Identify and attend schools that can sharpen your gifts into a first class talent. When your gift is sharpened into a first class gift, you will automatically become a first class human being. The only thing that can add value to your life is when you add value to your talents. This is achieved with proper education, training and practice.

Study hard and get best or good grades that can offer you admission into schools of your choice. If for any reason, you don't get admitted to schools of your choice; that is not the end of your life. Buy the best books and read and study them on your own. In the next five to ten years, the opportunities would come and you would have adequately prepared yourself enough to face life on your own. Herbert Harris was a renowned lawyer who served in the US attorney. He passed the New York State Bar exam without attending Law School. Take a cue from him.

Attend seminars, conferences and programs and always be prepared to learn new things especially, the ones that bother on your talents development. There are free seminars, conferences and programs that are being organized. If you genuinely don't have money to attend those that come with rate, endeavour to attend the free ones. You have nothing to lose but you have all to gain. Buy and read motivational books. Listen to inspirational messages. Watch videos that will empower you.

Make effective and efficient use of the internet and the social media. You need a lot of information to build your life but you don't need all information. Read only relevant information on the internet and social media. Read only positive information. Read only the ones that will develop you not the ones that will break you. Ignore negative information because they add no value to your life. They rather subtract from your life and steal treasures you used years to build in few days.

Be focused and concentrate on what you want to do with your talents. Be committed and dedicated to your calling. Let your talents rejuvenate your spirit man.

HOW TO INFLUENCE THE WORLD FROM YOUR GEOGRAPHICAL LOCATION

It is scientifically proven and universally accepted that the world is a globe which revolves on its axis causing the four seasonal changes; winter, spring, summer and autumn. It also rotates giving us day and night. The revolution takes a year to complete whilst the rotation completes in twenty four hours.

There are about ninety-five percent of the world's populations who behave in their thinking, decisions and actions as if the world is flat. They pathetically leave their homeland and travel to far towns, cities, countries, and even continents seeking for greener pastures, success, wealth, power and fame.

If you know that the world is a globe which rotates and revolves on its axis and completes the cycle every day and three hundred and sixty-five days respectively, you will fix and position yourself somewhere such that the entire world would have revolved and rotated underneath your feet someday to come. There is no need moving from place to place. You can affect the world from where you are. You can make any impact on the world from your place of dwelling. All you need is the talent and passion to do that.

Xavi Hernandez from Spain, Frank Lampard from England, and Mohammed Aboutrika from Egypt, have all not plied their football career outside their native country yet they have left legacy and made tremendous impact in their nation, continent and in world football.

Bill Gates, Steve Jobs, Warren Buffet and Mark Zuckerberg have not been to Ghana yet we hail them in Ghana. Mr. Kofi Annan positioned himself at a particular geographical location and controlled all the powers and governments of the world as the United Nations Secretary General.

THINK ABOUT THIS

I lead. I speak. I teach. I write. I preach. I analyze. I treat. I am creative.

I never knew I could lead people until I made the effort to lead. I never knew I could be a public speaker until I made the effort to speak in public. I had no idea I could teach until I made the decision to teach others. I had no knowledge I could write until I made a conscious decision to write medical articles to educate people. I was unaware I could preach until I made the decision to win more souls for Christ Jesus. I had no idea I could be an analyst until I started analyzing students results and policies. I never knew I could be creative until I started mind exercise and deep imaginations. I had no or limited knowledge on entrepreneurship until I ventured into it.

Wow…so God has endowed me with all these abilities and enablement (talents or gifts)? – Yes, He has. He has endowed you too with the same abilities or enablement. Yours may even be more than mine. The difference is maybe you have intentionally decided not to identify yours. Imagine how sad and disappointed God will feel if I failed to identify and utilize all these gifts. They will just lie dormant in me and remain unproductive. Are your talents lying dormant and unproductive? – Until you take that step or action…you will never realize your worth and what you have inside of you.

Each of my talents is enough to make me wealthy in life. Imagine if I combine all these talents, how much wealth will I be generating in just a year? Your guess is as good as mine. Take your time and nurture your talents and money, influence, power and all other goodies will chase you and knock at your door. "Talent is cheaper than table salt. What separates the talented individual from the successful one is a lot of hardwork." Stephen King remarked.

Identifying, knowing and developing your talents take you closer to understanding and fulfilling your life's purpose on the wheels or the passions you have.

UNDERSTANDING THE PURPOSE OF LIFE

"It is not the duration of your life, but the donation you make to life that matters."- Herbert Harris

PURPOSE

Your purpose is how and what you want your life to represent. It is revealed through your long-range goals. Your purpose provides orientation and direction for your journey through life. It is your reason for living. Like a ship's compass, your purpose guides you when all else fails. No one can choose your purpose for you. Only you can determine it for yourself. Your purpose is identified with the quality of your life. It is not how long you live, but rather what you do. It is not the duration of your life, but the donation you make to life that matters. What donation have you made to life so far? Many of the truly great achievers in history had relatively short lives. You must be obsessed with your purpose. Eat it, breathe it, think about it, and act on it every moment of every day. Live your life so that the use of your life will outlive your life.

HOW TO DEVELOP YOUR PURPOSE

According to one of American's great author and lawyer; Herbert Harris in his book, The 12 universal laws of success (p.73), there are six questions every well-meaning individual should keep asking himself within specific time interval. I don't just agree with him, but I practice it daily: Am I the person I really want to be? Am I living a meaningful life? What am I doing to realize a meaningful life? What am I doing to make my dreams and visions come true? What important contributions do I have to make to the world? What do I want my life to stand for?

In answering these questions, you must be honest with yourself. Do not deceive yourself. Take your time to analyse the questions with all seriousness and carefulness. Answers to these questions will not only shape your life pattern and rhythm; it will mould and direct your course towards a fulfilled destiny and earthly influence. The pattern for your life embraces the finite period from conception to death but the rhythm of your life embraces all eternity. Once you can articulate the answers to these questions, immediately develop a plan of action to implement your answers. When your patterns of life align with your rhythm, you change the course of history; improve the conditions of humanity, affect your world with truth, peace, deeper wisdom and understanding to the world.

HOW TO ESTABLISH YOUR PURPOSE

Your purpose must be idealistic. You must strive for the best in all things. Use your imagination to see things how they can or should be, rather than as they are. Your purpose must be visionary. Your purpose must be visionary means you must see beyond what others see, think beyond what others think and risk beyond what others think is safe. Try at all times to perceive, remember, accept and rely on your dreams. Not everyone around you will understand and accept your visions. Don't be surprised and discouraged if it appears or looks incomprehensible, impossible, unacceptable, impracticable and unrealistic to others. There are many of my friends who never supported me in some of my visions not because they hate or envy me, but because those visions appeared incomprehensible, impracticable and unrealistic to them. It is not strange if they don't support you.

Your purpose must be life-long. It is extremely difficult for life's purpose to change. However, your perception of it may change depending on your level of consciousness. Your purpose is your life's work which must be perceived and evaluated from moment to moment. If your purpose is lived well, it may extend well beyond the boundaries of your life-time. Your purpose must benefit everyone. A life lived for self is not worth living. A life lived for personal desires, ego and pride is a wasted life. You must live your life beyond yourself and ego. Once that happens, it will involve other people. This involvement must positively benefit all concerned. Your purpose must be challenging. It should stretch you to reach your highest potential. It should throw a continuous challenge to your faith and abilities. Your faith matures as your efforts yield expected results. As your faith grows, so does your ability to face and prevail over even greater challenges.

Your purpose must set you ablaze. In other words, your purpose must set you on an unquenchable fire. When your purpose sets you on an unquenchable fire, you become intoxicated and obsessed with its immediate and continuous realization. It permeates every tissue in your body and every fibre of your being radiates it. Every moment of your life, you incessantly think about it, talk about it. This fire originates from you deep rooted desire. Deep desires causes you to exert every element of power and energy you possess to achieve your purpose. Deep desire together with faith creates dynamic enthusiasm. Herbert Harris made it simple in these words, "Dynamic enthusiasm is the burning fire which stimulates your mental, physical, and psychic powers to the point where they become infectious, contagious, and invincible." Your purpose must be worthwhile. This implies that your purpose must accomplish or fulfil a legitimate positive need in the world. Take a pen and paper: write down your purpose. Act on it now! Don't wait!!!

LIFE WITHOUT A PURPOSE

The worst thing that can happen to anyone is to be living and does not know the purpose why he is alive. Sleep every night and wake up the next day to no purpose, is a tragedy of life. There are many people whose lives and destinies crashed because the purpose of life was not understood. No one will plan your life for you if you don't do it all by yourself. In order to understand the purpose of life, you must plan and create your future in imagination and work tirelessly towards achieving it. There are three major things that happen when life is not well planned and the purpose of life is not understood. When the purpose of life is not well planned and well understood:

1. life ends with regret
2. life is lived as a burden
3. disaster is inevitable

The day you take complete responsibility for yourself, the day you stop making any excuses, that's the day you start to the top – Unknown

WHEN PURPOSE IS NOT UNDERSTOOD

When the purpose of life is not well planned and well understood, the following occur.

1. LIFE ENDS WITH REGRET

There are many people who have regretted almost all steps they took or made in life simply because they never sat down to thoroughly assess the merits and demerits of making those steps. This ranges from regrets in failed financial ventures, educational careers, political endeavours and many others. It is normal to regret one or two decisions one has made in life, but when your regrets become too many, then check your planning skills. On the success way to personal growth, development and total financial freedom, decisions must be planned and well executed. You must understand why you were created by your Creator and as well fish out why you were born in this generation and no other generation. You have a divine assignment to undertake for the benefit of your family and your generation. You are very unique and special in the way God created you but your uniqueness becomes visible to the world only when you plan your visions and stick to achieving them no matter the challenges.

2. LIFE IS LIVED AS A BURDEN

There are several people who see life as more of a burden than enjoyment and fulfillment of divine assignment or calling. They have lost all hope and faith in themselves and in God and so they see life to be aimless and meaningless. Any time your regrets become more than you can bear, your positive perception about life changes. These victims now see life as aimless and meaningless, and that life has nothing good to offer them. They blame others for their woes. They feel bitter about the progress and success of their colleagues and they try to find ways of pulling them down. These people simply do not understand the purpose of life. They also lack the diligence to plan their life and execute those plans perfectly.

3. DISASTER IS INEVITABLE

These are failures in life who try to do things to harm themselves and others closer to them because they have lost total faith, hope and trust in their God and themselves as well and have decided to terminate their own lives. They are left with no other choice than to abruptly end their own lives because they have lost control. It is just like an aeroplane that has lost balance in the air some few minutes to its landing site. No matter how skilful the pilot may be, disaster will be inevitable. There are many people whose lives and destinies crashed because the purpose of life was not understood. It is very pathetic for such things to be recorded among God's children. Decision to commit suicide and its related activities can only be made by individuals who do not understand the purpose of life. When life is well planned and its purpose is explicitly stated and well understood in simple terms, even in times when the storm appears frightening and dangerous to sail through, and life is unexpectedly crashing on you from all angles, you will still remain fearless, steadfast and courageous because you have an anchor that holds and keeps your soul.

Let's visit Priscilla Jane Owens' hymn she wrote in 1882

"Will Your Anchor Hold" or "We Have an Anchor"

Will your anchor hold in the storms of life?

When the clouds unfold their wings of strife?

When the strong tides lift and the cables strain,

Will your anchor drift, or firm remain?

Refrain:

We have an anchor that keeps the soul

Steadfast and sure while the billows roll,

Fastened to the Rock which cannot move?

Grounded firm and deep in the Saviour's love

That's why David said *"even though I walk through the valley of the shadow of death, I will fear no evil, for you are with me; your rod and your staff, they comfort me" (Psalm 23:4)*

When the purpose of life is not understood, life crashes in a rush.

Do you know your purpose? Are you fulfilling your purpose? How will you know you are fulfilling your purpose? The way you live your life, does it please you? Does it please God as well? What is the quality of your life? How many people does your life benefit?

Knowing one's purpose brings result oriented visions and goals. It guides and directs you in the developments of your talents. It makes you focused on achieving set aims and objectives. It finally brings joy, success, and peace of mind, excellence, honour and reward.

Understanding your purpose exposes you to the facts of life. You must know and have these facts of life in order to excel.

THE FIVE (5) FACTS OF LIFE

In order to fully understand what life on earth is all about, it is paramount you know the facts of life. Knowing the facts of life will help you not only to understand it, but also to appreciate it and prepare adequately to meet its demands. The consciousness of these facts by an individual puts him/her at an advantageous position to mature and progress and succeed spiritually, economically, socially, mentally and physically. The Bible says for lack of knowledge my people perish. Many souls have perished and will continue to perish because of lack of knowledge and wisdom.

- **LIFE IS A GIFT**

"And he is not served by human hands, as if he needed anything, because he himself gives all men life and breath and everything else." (Acts 17:25)

Life is a gift means there is someone (a Supernatural Being) who gives life. In reading this book, you will fully awaken your awareness that your life is a gift from God. In this consciousness, plan, order and live your life in a way that will please the Giver. This is a universal gift given to the entire human race irrespective of your faith or beliefs. Nobody decided to live and he is alive.

A Gift is anything precious willingly given to someone without payment; a present. It can also be defined as a natural ability or talent. We have never paid and will never pay for the life we are living because it is a gift from God. We did nothing to deserve this gift. However, we have a duty to make sure the gift given us is properly handled with all carefulness and seriousness. The implication of life being a gift simply means, it must be lived to the pleasure of the Giver. The only way you can show gratitude to God for the life He has given you is to worship Him and live a meaningful life.

Even in this contemporary world, anytime we give a gift to our relatives, friends, mates or colleagues, we expect them to judiciously use these gifts. As human as we are, we feel pain, regret and disappointed if our gifts are not well appreciated and valued by the people we give those gifts to. Imagine you have bought an expensive suite as a gift for your friend and you later found it as a rug in his kitchen. What a waste of effort!!! The best gift you can give your children is education. Imagine you have sent your ward to the best school paying huge sum of fees and at the end of the day, he has woefully failed because he refused to study. What a pain!!!

God goes through the same pain and regret if we suffocate the life He has given us with immorality, greed, jealousy, hatred, adultery, corruption, pride, wickedness, alcoholism and the like. He regrets completely for creating you in the first place.

When men began to increase in number on the earth and daughters were born to them, the sons of God saw that the daughters of men were beautiful, and they married any of them they chose. Then the LORD said, "My Spirit will not contend with man forever, for he is mortal; his days will be a hundred and twenty years." The Nephilim were on the earth in those days—and also afterward—when the sons of God went to the daughters of men and had children by them. They were the heroes of old, men of renown. ***The LORD saw how great man's wickedness on the earth had become, and that every inclination of the thoughts of his heart was only evil all the time. The LORD was grieved that he had made man on the earth, and his heart was filled with pain.*** *So the LORD said "I will wipe mankind, whom I have created, from the face of the earth—men and animals, and creatures that move along the ground, and birds of the air—**for I am grieved that I have made them."** (Genesis 6:1-7) (NIV)*

However, God feels proud and happy when we live a pleasing life unto Him. His ears become more attentive to us and He constantly communicates with us through dreams, visions, and prophecies and blesses us with more gifts such as riches, success, joy, peace of mind, love, etc. We can learn from Noah, Abraham, Jacob, Job, David, Solomon, et cetera from the Bible.

Please pause and ask yourself this question and genuinely answer it. Any time, any day, any moment when God looks down the earth from heaven, will He rejoice or regret ever creating you because of your secret deeds? Note this: on judgment day, every secret will be made public, so don't have too many secrets. Think deep before answering this question. If yes…it is not too late…it is possible to make amends now so you can live the Godly life you have always desired.

It is forgetfulness of true identity and nature that makes people do what they do in our society.

- **LIFE IS GRACE**

Life is grace or a privilege and not a right. Grace is simply an unmerited favour. Grace is a privilege we have been giving, not a right. We don't merit the life we are living, yet we are alive because of God's abundant grace. Anytime you sleep and wake up healthy the next day, thank your God because it is not your right to wake up wholly fit. You are privileged to have woken up and counted among the living. Some people slept in good health but woke up in death the following day. For you to wake up today, it is never your might neither is it your prayers but the divine grace and mercies of Elohim. You have made several travels to far and near places yet you were never involved in any mild or fatal accident. Some people have travelled less than the number of your travels, yet they had accident and died or have become disabled. You think it was your prayers. Brethren it is never your efforts or prayers. It is God's divine protection and travelling mercies upon your life. You have been driving for the past five or ten years and you never had any accident and you think you are very skilful. Stop deceiving yourself. Praise your Maker for that privilege.

You are very wealthy and you and your family have never been attacked by armed robbers before and you think you have a tight security system or personnel. People have much tighter security system and personnel than you yet they were attacked and killed. God have mercy! It is the love of God that has brought you this far. You had severe malaria or severe febrile condition and you were cured and you think your doctor is the one who saved your life. Meanwhile another patient with uncomplicated malaria died in the hands of that same doctor. Don't forget that it was the Lord's divine healing power. You survived labour and caesarean section respectively in your two deliveries and you think it was your own effort and that of the midwives and the doctors. Yet pregnant women die in the hands of these same healthcare providers almost every week. Even doctors who treat patients die too. It is the Lord's divine hands and nothing else.

Your business is flourishing not because you are a smart financial analyst and strategist but it's because God has decided to bless and give you good success. There are others, who are smarter and richer than you, yet their businesses collapsed and they went bankrupt. It is a privilege. You are doing well in your field of endeavour and making it big in your social, professional, political, spiritual and economic life because God has given you that privilege. Anytime you have the opportunity of seeing and welcoming a new day, thank God for that privilege because thousands of people were denied that opportunity and privilege. If you know and walk in this consciousness and reality that life is indeed grace or a privilege, you will always be appreciative and grateful to God on daily basis.

My increasing medical knowledge and research has made me to appreciate the works and wonders of God the more. I have been exposed to several medical conditions that have no known causes. These conditions are mostly autoimmune (self-destruction) diseases that can attack any living being as far as he or she remains on the earth. These diseases are very dangerous and deadly. God has been faithful for His mercies, loving kindness and protection upon our lives against these diseases. Life is a privilege. Show gratitude and appreciation to God at every moment when you have the breath of life. Life is grace or a privilege means it must never be taken for granted. It must be lived with appreciation.

"No one can be too powerful and for the sake of his power he's alive, no one can be so wise and because of his wisdom he's alive, no one can be too connected and his connection made him to live, no one can be so talented and because of his talent, he's alive, no one can be so rich and because of his wealth, he's alive, no one can be so intelligent and knowledgeable and for the sake of his intelligence and knowledge, he's alive. For every second a man lives, it is a privilege and not a right." – Pastor Dr. Paul Enenche

---

- **LIFE IS A SEED**

Do not be deceived: God cannot be mocked. A man reaps what he sows. (Galatians 6:7)

Life is a seed. Any deed or action you take in life whether good or bad is a seed you have sown which will germinate and produce fruits for harvest. The way you live is seeds you are sowing. Your living is your seeding. Whatever you sow today so shall you reap tomorrow. Your living will determine where you will be in time and eternity. Your decisions and actions today will determine where you will end tomorrow. Your choice of meal today and your lifestyle determines your health tomorrow. The Chief Pathologist in Ghana; Professor Badu Akorsa advised that about 80% of deaths are preventable just with appropriate diet modification. Every act is a seed that is definitely going to produce a harvest. Your relationship with your fellow human beings: your character, your lifestyle, your utterances, your demeanour, your attitude and habit; they are seeds you are sowing today that is definitely going to produce harvest in time and eternity. How you live in time determines where you will end in eternity. Beware how you live because your living is your seeding.

Any time you lied against your fellow human being at the place of work so you can gain favour, you have sown a seed that you will reap in time and eternity. Any time you have accepted bribe in order to pervert justice, you have sown a seed that you will reap in time and eternity. Remember how Anas Aremeyaw Anas recently exposed the corrupt practices of some Ghanaian Judges. Most implicated Judges have paid for their act painfully. It serves them right!!! Any time you have committed fornication and adultery, you have sown a seed that you will reap in time and eternity. Any time you have failed a student in examination because he/she has failed to compromise or sleep with you, you have sown a seed that you will reap in time and eternity. As if they have brought them to school for you to destroy their lives. Any time you smoke or drink or murder, you have sown a seed that you will reap in time and eternity. Any act of wickedness you have committed against your fellow human being, you have sown a seed that you will reap in time and eternity. Any time you snatch someone's wife or husband from the rightful owner, you have sown a seed that you will reap in time and eternity. There are people who do things today and implicate their children, even children yet unborn. They do things that their children may not recover from the consequences of those acts or deeds.

"When Gehazi came to the hill, he took the things from the servants and put them away in the house. He sent the men away and they left. Then he went in and stood before his master Elisha. "Where have you been Gehazi?" Elisha asked. "Your servant didn't go anywhere," Gehazi answered. But Elisha said to him, "Was not my spirit with you when the man got down from his chariots to meet you? Is this the time to take money (bribe), or to accept clothes, olive groves, vineyards, flocks, herds, or men servants and maid servants? ***Naaman's leprosy will cling to you and to your descendants forever." Then Gehazi went from Elisha's presence and he was leprous, as white as snow.*** *" (2nd Kings 5:1-27)*

The frequency of persistently sowing negative seeds on daily basis will result in harvesting multiple complicated problems and frustrations.

Any time you put a smile on someone's face or release intellectual and financial resources to bless someone's life or support the work of God, you have sown a seed that you will reap in time and eternity. Any time you intercede for someone in prayers or you do something good for your fellow human being, you have sown a seed that you will reap in time and eternity. Any time you stand and insist on doing the right thing or motivate someone, you have sown a seed that you will reap in time and eternity. Endeavour to sow good seeds.

The frequency of persistently sowing positive seeds on daily basis will result in harvesting joy, success, peace of mind, power and excellence. Your daily or weekly write ups or posts on social media (Facebook, Twitter, WhatsApp, Instagram, Blog, and Internet) are seeds that you are sowing. Beware what you post because people are watching and monitoring you closely without your notice. Recently, one of my friends got a multimillion US Dollar deal that has forever changed his life. You know how he got it? He never had it because of his educational qualification or whatsoever; he had it because of his daily motivational posts on Facebook. That was all!!! However, a young Ghanaian guy was arrested and jailed recently because he published a post on Facebook threatening to kill the American Ambassador to Ghana if given the chance. You see what social media can offer you? It's all about the type of seed you sow.

A seed grows with no sound, but a tree falls with a huge noise. Destruction has noise, but creation is silent. In your success, remain silent as there is power in silence. Grow silently and allow the master Jesus Christ to shape you.

Life is a seed, endeavour to sow good seeds.

- **LIFE IS LIKE A GAME**

Life is a game. It is like a game of football, volley ball, table tennis, boxing, and the like. Just as a lot of physical, spiritual and psychological preparations are made before the commencement of any game event, so is life. There is a way to prepare to win games and there is also a way to prepare to lose games. In the same vein, there is a way to live to win and there is also a way to live to lose. Living determines winning and living determines losing. The way you live your life determines whether you will succeed or fail. Everybody has equal amount of time in a day but the way you use your time determines whether you maximize it or not.

How you spend your time, energy and resources determines your success or failure. How prepared are you for the game of life? What do you use your financial resources for? What do you use your energy for? What do you use your time for? Is what you are gaining worth over what you are losing?

At the end of every game, there are results. The results justify the game. The justification shows your preparations before and during the game. You cannot lose the game of life. You must always play to win. How do you do that? Use your time wisely. There is no time to waste. Channel your energy to things you can do best (ambitions) and do them with excellence if not perfection. Spend your money wisely. Invest your money in your ambitions and polish your talent. Explore business ventures. Prepare and equip yourself adequately with the principles governing the game of life.

I heard a story of a man who was drunk and riding a motorbike in the night which had no light and no break. The night was a Christmas day night. What a game!!! Maybe he had played it before and won but not on that day. He ran into an oncoming Mercedes Benz and died on the spot. He played to lose. He lost in time and lost eternally in eternity.

Don't play the game of life recklessly because it's only once. Don't drive recklessly and die out of an avoidable accident. Don't follow pleasure and contract STDs (HIV/AIDS). The pleasure you got, does it justify the HIV? Don't follow money and die prematurely. Don't be a lazy student and fail your exams. Don't follow friends and become a slave to immorality, alcoholism, smoking and other social vices. Do not consume any meal just for the sake of satisfying your hunger. It may cost you dearly tomorrow. Esau lived to lose. Jacob lived to win. Esau got the meal of a day and lost his right of a lifetime. (Genesis 27)

Life is a game, my counsel is, play to win

- **LIFE IS A VAPOUR**

"Why, you do not even know what will happen tomorrow. What is your life? You are a mist (vapour) that appears for a little while and then vanishes." James 4:14 (NIV)

Everyone you see today will go some day. For it is appointed unto man to die once, after that judgment. (Hebrews 9:27). Life is a vapour implies that we will never live forever. Each of us has a temporal and a very short duration to live in this world. There is an appointed time when you will be called to eternity. Steven Jobs died at the age of 54. He was the father and founder of "Apple Computers". He said he was going to give a talk at the university when he noticed, felt, and realized a terminal symptom in his body. He gave the talk for only fifteen minutes and headed to the hospital to see his doctor. He said the very moment the doctor showed him his diagnosis; the whole of his life came before him and three paramount questions came to his mind. "How did I live? How should I have lived? What should I do?" Then he went on to advice that, "Live each day as if it is the last because one day it will be the last" This is not to frighten you to say you will die tomorrow but to make you live on the urge. Life is too short to joke around.

Someone asked John Wesley; the founder of the Methodist Church that "If you have only tomorrow (24 hours) to live, what would you do?" He said "I will continue to do exactly what I'm doing now. There is nothing I would have loved to do that I'm not currently doing. I am living my life the way I should live it" Live with the sense of urgency. Understand your priorities and understand your posteriorities. Know what to put in front of you and know what to put behind you. Do not bother yourself with what does not matter. Do not spend your life making enemies. Life is too short to be spent on making enemies. Make friends rather than enemies.

The Book of Ecclesiastes Chapter 3 tells us that there is time for everything under the sun. What will the world, the continent, your country, region, district, society, community, your family, colleague workers, company or institution, your school mates, friends remember you for? What legacy do you intend leaving behind?

HOW TO LIVE AN EXCELLENT LIFE

With the facts of life in mind, there are three major things you must do if you are poised to reaching excellence and eventually getting to the top successfully with ease: You must ensure quality continual relationship with God, you must ensure quality relationship with humanity, and you must make quality impact. How do you make these happen?

ENSURE QUALITY CONTINUAL RELATIONSHIP WITH GOD

Make an unwavering attempt and effort to live a life that is permanently pleasing your Maker who is the Giver of your life. Study His word daily, pray to Him always and have faith in Him. Your resources are released to you from a Supernatural Source. Your life must not get disconnected from its original Source. When there is disconnection between life and Source, resources cannot be provided or received from the Source. Life is a privilege so be appreciative and thankful to God in all circumstances.

ENSURE QUALITY RELATIONSHIP WITH HUMANITY

This model is not to say, you should please others at the expense of your own happiness and joy. It's to emphasis the fact that, don't spend your entire life making enemies. Don't be a person full of enemies. When this happens, check your life and quickly make amends. You may be wrong in most of your dealings with humanity. Ensure that quality relationship exists between you and the people around you in any way possible. Be more of people person and not an anti-people person. After all, life is a vapour which appears for a while and after which it vanishes away. Life is too short to concentrate on making enemies for yourself. Concentrate on making healthy relationship with people. Leave enemy creation for the untrained, uncivilized and uncultured people. Refuse to join them!

ENSURE YOU MAKE QUALITY IMPACT

Live your life in a way that will benefit humanity. Let somebody be happy because your mother gave birth to you. Don't spend your time making enemies. Spend your time making friends and impacting your world around you. Make an impact on your society. Be a man of solutions but not a man of problems. Stretch into your inner wealth and bring out all that God has blessed you with for the sake of humanity. Leave an indelible mark in the hearts of many. Many people's success and life depend on you so never disappoint them. Ensure you make quality impact in your family, place of work, in your profession, in your nation, community, continent, and the world at large.

Don't be afraid to change and refocus if you feel you don't know any or all your talents and you are not pursuing your purpose as well. Don't be afraid to change your mentality after knowing the facts of life.

CHANGE IS A SIGN OF MATURITY

"I was once an armed robber"- Archbishop Duncan Williams

Developmentalists and Human Growth Analysts through thorough research and analysis have found out and concluded that there are three critical stages of every living being from conception through to death. It is believed that these stages are so critical and crucial such that maximum attention and protection are needed in each stage of growth and development. These specialists take into account the cellular, hormonal, and internal and somewhat invisible chemical reactions and transformations that occur in living organisms which eventually manifest in external alterations of their body structure and outlook.

THE FIRST TWO WEEKS OF LIFE

The first stage is the first two weeks of life. This part of life is entirely spent in the womb of the woman. These are the first two weeks immediately after fertilization is confirmed or has occurred. In such conditions, the pregnant woman is advised never to take drugs and medications not prescribed by a qualified medical professional. She is also warned against introducing unhygienic and dangerous chemicals into her vagina. These things may not be necessarily dangerous or poisonous to the woman, but may be very toxic to the developing zygote. And for this reason, she must obey these instructions if she wants to deliver a sound healthy baby. This is the stage where the zygote undergoes rapid and progressive cell division in order to implant or attach itself to the appropriate walls of the uterus.

These cells migrate to their appropriate places where they start to form the vital body organs. This requires a conducive and serene environment for these cellular activities to take place in order to achieve desired growth and result. That is to say, the fused gametes can only grow after they have changed in form and in composition or make up. This transformation can only take place in a hormonally balanced environment. It means; no change, no growth. Any external or hormonal disturbances could halt, delay and destroy the process. The zygote is so fragile such that any small disturbance or unfavourable condition promotes its death or extinction. This explains why less than two weeks old zygote can easily be aborted with the slightest mistake. Even if the zygote survives, there is a high possibility of giving birth to someone with genetic disorder or a physically challenged being. Scientifically, the human heart and other major organs start developing and functioning immediately after two weeks of life in utero.

THE FIRST TWO YEARS AFTER BIRTH

The second stage is the first two years after birth. According to Developmentalists, there is a high survival rate of a child against most childhood diseases after age two (2). In the first six months, the mother is expected to exclusively breastfeed the baby. This gives maternal immunity to the child and thereby, preventing childhood illnesses. After the six months, the child is to be fed with highly nutritious meal for proper nourishment so that the earlier immunity built will be maintained and improved. Proper hygienic conditions must always be maintained in and around the environment of the child. These are practices that keep the child safe for growth to be possible. The baby undergoes various changes from rolling in bed, sitting up in bed, crawling, walking, talking and eating. As these developmental changes are occurring, the muscles grow in proportionate measure and the muscle tone keeps increasing and supporting child's activities. These changes are very crucial for growth to occur.

THE ADOLESCENT STAGE

Many authors and literature have used varying age groups in their presentation on the age range for adolescents. But I believe adolescents are boys in the teen age whilst adolescent girls are from eleven years to nineteen. This is the last stage. Adolescents become vulnerable to various social vices such as smoking, alcoholism, immorality, rebellion, etc. They are not able to control their sexual desires and pleasures because of the hormonal changes occurring in their system. If care is not taken in this period of life, the adolescent can contract life-threatening infections that may affect his/her life permanently. Again, parents are advised to be vigilant because these internal and external changes in their children can lead to a desired maturity or otherwise.

All these three stages discussed involve changes that lead to growth or maturity and transition from one phase of life to another. There must always be a change to ensure growth and development in a particular direction. Without change, there can't be growth and development. Without growth and development, there is no progress. Without change, there is stagnation. Life stinks when there is stagnation! Imagine a foetus in the womb that fails to change and grow. It means death has occurred. With time, the dead foetus begins to decay. It starts to emit unbearable odour through the uterine and vaginal secretions in utero causing a lot of complications to its carrier. Without change, life is meaningless. Growth and maturity can never be reversible. In much the same way, change should not be reversible. It should not bring retrogression!

THE CATERPILLAR AND THE BUTTERFLY

A beautiful butterfly can't develop without becoming a caterpillar first. And a caterpillar becomes useless if it doesn't eventually evolve to become a butterfly. Before an ugly wingless caterpillar becomes a beautiful lovely winged butterfly, it undergoes series of painful metamorphosis (pupal stage) to the extent that it is perceived as if it is dead. It is only in that perceived "dead" state (pupal stage) that it can become that wonderful butterfly that flies around. When the caterpillar undergoes that change and finally becomes a butterfly, it is a sign of maturity. It is an indication that the butterfly is matured to face life on its own. Change is a sign of maturity. Any change that does not bring maturity is not a good change.

WHAT HAPPENS TO THE EAGLE @ AGE FORTY

The eagle known as the king of all birds has shown us the relevance of undergoing changes. Researchers about the eagle have observed that at around age 40, the eagle's claws and beak become very weak such that the eagle is unable to catch its preys and feed on them. This means if the eagle does nothing about its situation, it may die as a result of hunger. The eagle therefore, undergoes a painful exercise and change for several days by hiding in a comfortable hide out where it removes its claws and beak. It then, patiently, waits for many days for new claws and beak to grow. After they have fully grown, the eagle comes back to full force and lives for the next 30 years or so. The change has made it possible for new claws and beak to grow. This in effect makes the eagle to grow and mature more than other eagles that may not be able to go through that process. Again, it is evident that change causes growth and maturity.

THIS IS IMPORTANT; NOTE IT

Apart from the three critical human changes discussed in this concept earlier, it is important to know this powerful truth as well. The human body undergoes changes every seven (7) years. Your body's outlook, your ideas, behaviors, attitudes, likes and dislikes, and the way you perceive and interpret things change every seven years. In the next seven years, you wouldn't have the same ideas, behaviours, and the attitudes you have today. Your outlook will be totally different. You will completely change either for good or bad depending on what you have socialized yourself with. Change is natural. Don't restrict it but you can tailor it in a positive direction.

RENEW YOUR MIND

"Do not conform any longer to the patterns of this world, but be transformed by the renewing of your mind. Then you will be able to test and approve what God's will is—his good, pleasing and perfect will" (Roman 12:2)

There are three things that bring change in our life experiences. These are faith, desire and choice. ***Faith is what brings unseen or invisible things to the visible world.*** If you have the faith that your troubles, challenges, and situation will change for the better someday to come, it will truly happen in your life. Change your ways by renewing your mind towards positivity. You can't renew your mind if you don't have faith. Until Nicholas Duncan William (the then armed robber) had faith in God and renewed his mind towards a positive change, he would have languished in the armed robbery business for life. Just take a pause and look at the many sons Archbishop Nicholas Duncan William has nurtured for Kingdom work; Eastwood Anaba, Dag Heward Mills, Sam Korankye Ankra, etc. Imagine how many lives his sons have touched. Again, imagine how many lives his sons' sons have also touched. The imagination continues in that order. This is how you will also affect humanity if you make the decision to renew your mind and have faith that God can use you for greater works.

You must have a ***burning desire*** to change your current situation or circumstance. Until your situation changes for the better, you don't stop. To refuse to change is to live with the old mentality. To live with the old mentality is to live in the past. To live in the past is move your life in retrogression. And to move your life in retrogression is a sign that you are not growing. To live without growth, is denial of faith and heavenly mandate.

We are confronted with choices every single minute in every single day. Anything in life comes with choice. We make the choice whether consciously or unconsciously based on our perception about the situation or the challenge. This occurs in our mind world. For you to change your life for the better, you must convincingly identify and specifically define what a better life means to you. And you must choose to pursue this better life you have defined for yourself, and make the changes in your thinking and action that will bring it about. In Luke 15:11-32, until the prodigal son desired to get back home and made the ***choice*** to come back home to reconcile with his father, he would have died out of hunger and intense suffering. He did this by merely changing his thought and realizing how stupid he had been in his old thoughts. His definition of a better life didn't correspond with the environment he found himself in and so there was a need for him to reconcile with his father so that he can live his better life.

Society, organizations, institutions and schools can only become better and develop if the people concerned have ***opted*** for a positive change in behaviour, lifestyle, and beliefs and embrace the fact that it is only that change that can bring the results they so much desire. This is called ***choice***. Until you make a good choice, don't expect development and growth or maturity. ***Societies and institutions can only develop when the people involve have developed a sense of development.***

CHALLENGES CONFRONTING CHANGE

The main challenge confronting change is fear. Fear doesn't actually exist. We give it place and the freedom for it to exist in our world mind. If you sow the seed of fear, it germinates, gains roots and grows slowly. In no time, it matures and becomes a monster that disturbs your life for years. It limits your potential and prevents you from becoming the personality God created you to be. Fear presents itself in the following ways:

1. ***Fear of change***
2. ***Fear of criticism***
3. ***Fear of failure***

Don't be afraid to change because everyone must go through periodic changes in order to go through life peacefully. Don't fear criticism because most of the time, it is actually a compliment in disguise. Don't fear failure because it is part of life. ***Treat fear as weed in your beautiful garden of life. Remove the weed without thinking twice about it. Eliminate the weed at all cost because it prevents bumper harvest.***

Change is a natural principle God used in creating the earth. Let's ponder over these:

Tadpole living in water changes into toad which then lives on land. Adult toads live on land most of the time and rely on water for hydration, breeding, and temperature regulation. As they get older, tadpoles begin to develop legs and lungs and they will reabsorb their tails and gills. They will look more like adult anurans and they will eventually live on dry land. The deep lesson in this is that, any time you have undergone certain changes in life, it is needless and sometimes suicidal to stay in your former zone. You must move to a higher dimension in correspondence with the change you have undergone in order to properly cope with life.

In the world of lions, gestation, the period of time in which the young are carried and develop in the mother's uterus, lasts for 105 to 118 days. When a cub is born, it is ***blind*** and lives off its mother's milk. It gains sight during the first 11 days and learns to walk after two weeks. In the fourth week, milk teeth develop and the cubs learn to run. The cub is weaned from milk when it is 10 months old and grows its permanent teeth. Between its first and second year, the cub makes its first kill. Even the cub (young lion) is born blind yet it undergoes changes to become the king of the jungle.

Some species of sharks lay eggs in the sea with the developing embryo covered by a tough, protective case. This is known as oviparous reproduction. The embryos of these sharks are well supplied with nutritious yolk, unlike the tiny eggs of most bony fish. After some time, the egg hatches and a young shark emerges. This type of reproduction exposes the eggs to predators and many of the eggs are therefore mostly consumed because of the hostile environment. But the few eggs that undergo change (hatch) eventually become the king of the fishes.

Just as the eagle (king of birds) painfully changes its beak and claws, the lion (king of the jungle) is born blind, some species of shark (king of fishes) undergo oviparous reproduction, but eventually become rulers in their domain and kingdom, we as human beings must also accept the challenges associated with change and embrace it in good faith. When we allow ourselves to freely undergo the needed change, we will mature and progressively reach our highest potential in life.

There are certain things beyond your control. You can't change the economy. You can't alter the trends in the world. The societal values are so entrenched to adjust. It is difficult to change other human beings. But you certainly can change yourself holistically if you want to mature.

THE NOKIA LESSON

During the press conference to announce NOKIA being acquired by Microsoft, Nokia CEO ended his speech by saying this "we didn't do anything wrong, but somehow, we lost". Upon saying that, all his management team, himself included, teared sadly. Nokia has been a respectable company. They didn't do anything wrong in their business, however, the world changed too fast. Their opponents were too powerful. They missed out on learning, they missed out on changing, and thus they lost the opportunity at hand to make it big. Not only did they miss the opportunity to earn big money, they lost their chance of survival.

The message is crystal clear, if you don't change, you shall be removed from the competition. It's not wrong if you don't want to learn new things. However, if your thoughts and mindset cannot catch up with time, you will be eliminated. The advantage you had yesterday will be replaced by the trends of tomorrow. You don't have to do anything wrong, as long as your competitors catch the wave and do them right, you can lose out and fail.

To change and improve your self is giving yourself a second chance. To be forced by others to change, is like being thrown out. Those who refuse to learn and improve will definitely one day become redundant and irrelevant to their field. They will learn the lesson in a hard and expensive way! Keep learning. Keep innovating. Stay relevant.

Change doesn't happen in any human endeavour unless there is change of mentality and renewal of thoughts. Use the renewed mind well because change has brought in you a new mindset and mentality. The time is now to think and affect everything around you positively!

HOW THOUGHTS BECOME EMOTIONS

"As a single footstep will not make a path on the earth, so a single thought will not make a pathway in the mind. To make a deep physical path, we walk again and again. To make a deep mental path, we must think over and over the kind of thoughts we wish to dominate our lives." - Henry David Thoreau

You cannot chase and pursue excellence without due adherence to some seven key principles in successful living. These principles are such that once you begin with the first principle, you must with the same energy and enthusiasm with which you started the first one, strategically, follow through to the very last (seventh) principle. The first two principles have been discussed in this chapter. The remaining five have been explained in the next chapter. People with the eagle mindset will do all what it takes to reach the top. The top is spacious and convenient to accommodate all but the point is it is not for chickens but eagles. It is only the people with the attributes of an eagle who can distinguish themselves in this world.

People with the eagle mindset think about the future and create it with their imagination; they cognitively feel the emotions that come with tomorrow's excellence; these emotions are immediately put into visions and written down in simple applicable terms, goals are gotten from the visions to narrow it, strategic plans are developed to work on the goals, appropriate actions are taken to diligently execute the plans, and excellent results are inevitable. This is how thoughts become results. Refuse to think and behave like a chicken. The eagle remains the most powerful bird of all birds, think like it and act like it and the sky will remain your limit.

- **THE POWER OF YOUR THOUGHTS**

You are essentially who you create yourself to be and all that occurs in your life is the result of your own thinking. -Stephen Richards

The beginning of success or failure rides on the back of the principle of our thoughts. Think right. Think positive. Think excellence. Think big. Think beyond mediocrity. Think outside ordinariness. Think wealth. Think eternal victory. Create how you want your life to be in this world with your thoughts and imagination. Refuse to look down on yourself. You are greater than you think. Broaden the scope of your self-image. You are God's image and His ambassador on earth. God never fails so His children never fail. God has given you dominion over all things.

Command things with your thoughts and they will bow to you. You have a well of wealth, power, energy, influence, excellence deposited inside of you. Get up and stir it up now. It has been dormant for far too long. The right time is now. There is no other time than now. I perfectly agree with Napoleon Hill when he said "Don't wait; the time will never just be right."

Success will never lower its standards to accommodate you. You have to raise your standards to achieve it. God provides food for every bird but not in their nests. Rise up to the challenges ahead of you and conquer your fears. Let your greatest fear be the fact that you are powerful beyond measure and well-endowed within. Think differently from how the masses think. The masses think mediocrity and ordinariness. The masses protect and maintain the status quo. Refuse to join them. You will become a slave to the status quo and ordinary things if you join them. Henry David Thoreau was right when he said, "As a single footstep will not make a path on the earth, so a single thought will not make a pathway in the mind. To make a deep physical path, we walk again and again. To make a deep mental path, we must think over and over the kind of thoughts we wish to dominate our lives."

WHAT KINDS OF THOUGHTS DOMINATE YOUR LIFE?

No wonder Bruce Barton observed "Nothing splendid has ever been achieved except by those who dared believe that something inside them was superior to circumstance." The future began yesterday and we are already late. None other than ourselves can change our mind. Be a big picture thinker. It is brains that develop nations; not natural resources. Learn, unlearn and re-learn. That is how you can overcome challenges. Every problem is an opportunity. There is a message in every mess and an opportunity in every negative experience.

"You are the Michelangelo of your own life. The David that you are sculpting is you. And you do it with your thoughts". Joe Vitale

---

The Supreme Law of Change states "You can change who you are by changing what you put into your mind" This law is irrevocable and unavoidable. It is constantly present and controls the outcome of one's life. Change for the better. "Renew your mind", so the Holy Book says. Have a positive mental image of your being. No one will believe in you first except yourself. You are never inferior in the sight of God. You are a conqueror, a warrior and a winner. Never accept people's definitions about your abilities and capabilities. Accept your own definition about your abilities and capabilities and that alone is enough to motivate and propel you to reach your limit.

Bob Marley once said, "Life is one big road with lots of signs. So when you are riding through the ruts, don't complicate your mind. Flee from hate, mischief and jealousy. Don't bury your thoughts; put your vision to reality. Wake up and live." Have you complicated your mind with unnecessary, greedy and/or inferior thoughts? Have you buried the thoughts that can make you progress, prosper and have dominion in life? Or you have put them to sleep? Wake up brethren, the world awaits powerful manifestation of your thoughts and handiworks.

Thoughts such as: I want to be a renowned Gynaecologist, I want to be a Lecturer, I want to be professional Journalist, I want to be CEO of a renowned company, I want to be a respectable Politician, I want to be a Reverend Minister, I want to be an Administrator, I want to be a world class Sportsman, I want to be an enviable Entrepreneur, et cetera. Thoughts when nurtured and watered well germinate and mature into ambitions.

Life is full of choices. Any decision or choice you make in life has its direct implications and results. Think positive and make the right choices. Norman Vincent Peale observed "Believe in yourself! Have faith in your abilities! Without a humble but reasonable confidence in your own powers you cannot be successful or happy."

- **HOW THOUGHTS BECOME FEELINGS/EMOTIONS**

Our thoughts are communicated to our hearts and that produces feelings or emotions. Your emotions are results of your thoughts. Emotions are reactions that come with our thoughts. How strong your emotions are depends on the depth of your thought. Our thoughts have three different depths they get to and each level or depth determines the power of our thoughts. The deeper you go, the more powerful your thoughts and the more emotional and passionate you become about those thoughts. These levels are the conscious mind, the subconscious mind and the superconscious mind.

THE CONSCIOUS MIND

The conscious mind processes the everyday thoughts we make. Every thought has two distinct characteristics; the idea (the statement of the thought) and the feeling (emotions accompanying the thought). Your conscious mind transmits your thoughts to your subconscious mind through the feeling aspect of the thought. The conscious mind proceeds to conclusions based on observation, experience, and education. It is selective and judgmental. It represents the world of effect.

THE SUBCONSCIOUS MIND

The subconscious mind represents what you are and it is your emotional, feeling mind. It receives all ideas from the conscious mind and gives them form and expression through feeling. Your subconscious mind accepts every idea as true and gives it meaning, form and expression through feeling. The subconscious mind operates on the assumption of truth of every idea, and develops a series of systems which will manifest that truth in accord with the feelings associated with the thoughts. It is non-selective and non-judgmental. It represents the world of cause.

THE SUPERCONSCIOUS MIND

The superconscious mind remains the source of all creativity and faith. It is your spiritual mind operating on a subconscious level in all moments and at all times. It has complete, total and perfect access to all ideas, feelings and all intricate information recorded in your subconscious mind. Herbert Harris described the superconscious mind in the following terms, "It has unlimited access to all knowledge and information in existence."

The superconscious mind is the origin of all inspiration, intuition and intrinsic motivation. It brings goal-oriented motivation, and is stimulated by clarity of thought and decisiveness of actions. The superconscious mind has powerfully powerful power because it responds to clear concise authoritative commands by releasing ideas and energy. Your superconscious mind does not differentiate between times; it is independent of time. Yesterday (the past), today (the present), and tomorrow (the future) are one and the same. It is identified with the God Mind.

The summary is that, you have a thought in your conscious mind. The emotional aspect of this thought stimulates the subconscious mind, which then communicates and interacts with the superconscious mind to manifest the thought in your life experiences.

There are several people who operate only up to the conscious mind level. Their thoughts never give them any feelings. There are those who also operate only up to the subconscious level. Their thoughts give them emotions but these emotions do not have the enthusiasm and the zeal to stimulate the superconscious mind. There are only a few people who are constantly operating in the superconscious mind level. These people are the difference makers. **The truth is that thoughts can only become realities or results after they have reached the superconscious mind level.** You can as well call these depths as "The Consciousness Level".

HOW EMOTIONS BECOME RESULTS

You must read chapter seven in order to appreciate the explanations and the teachings in this chapter. The content in this chapter is separated from the preceding chapter because these five principles are the major operational pillars of success. Concentration is therefore needed on them if we want to be part of the peak performers in our endeavours.

- **HOW EMOTIONS BECOME VISIONS**

"Where there is no vision, there is no hope." -George Washington Carver

A thought (dream) written down with a date becomes a vision. And a vision smartly narrowed down is a goal. A goal broken down into steps becomes a plan. A plan backed by action makes your dream a reality. After you have thought and felt it in the superconscious mind, the next step is to write down your vision about the thought. In every single thought or dream, there is an accompanied and proportional vision that needs to be immediately written down with a date. This requires wisdom in order to get a clearer vision from your thoughts. Wisdom is the principal thing. Pray for wisdom on daily basis and you shall have it.

Vision gives you a sense of direction and focus. Vision gives you a clear picture of your thoughts. Vision makes you perceive the possibilities of your thoughts. Vision gives you proper understanding and a sense of urgency and a call to duty. It makes you restless and gives you sleepless nights. A vision is just transferring a raw thought onto paper awaiting further division into goals. Visions streamline your life and give you a sense of responsibility and discipline. One of the greatest turning points in the journey to the top is to have vision. Many lives and destinies crushed and perished because there was no vision. Thinking alone is not enough. Thinking and have feelings alone is not enough. Transfer your thoughts and feelings onto paper and write a date attached to it. The date reminds you of the time and moment when God gave you the thought.

It is free to think and have feelings as a result of your thoughts. But it takes wisdom, discipline and effort to write down your thoughts. It is expensive to have vision because that distinguishes you from the ordinary man and puts you among the expensive class of human beings. Vision puts you on the journey to the top. Your value starts increasing the very moment you start having visions and working towards achieving them. It is vision and dedication to accomplishing the vision that separates the men from the boys. **Men have visions, boys just think and dream dreams.** Don't just think and dream dreams because every ordinary man thinks and dreams. Have vision. Chase your vision. Don't just dream. Convert your dream to a vision. Convert thoughts in your superconscious mind to visions. It is visions that transform the world not just mere thoughts. Thoughts escape into thin air within few days. Visions remain with you forever.

Any thought well-articulated on paper awaiting manifestation and implementation is a vision. A vision should be clear, concise and very simple to understand. Examples include; I would be a renowned Gynaecologist, I would be a Lecturer, I would be professional Journalist, I would be CEO of a renowned company, I would be a respectable Politician, I would be a Reverend Minister, I would be an Administrator, I would be a world class Sportsman, I would be an enviable Entrepreneur, et cetera. Visions metamorphose into ambitions.

Walk your vision. Confess your vision. Act your vision. Reflect your vision. Radiate your vision. Let every aspect of your life communicate your vision. Former President of Ghana His Excellency John Agyekum Kuffour had this to say, "I told my school mates I'll be a President, they started using that to tease me, 'Mr. President! Mr. President!!" You can see that he conceived the vision of becoming a President of Ghana during his school days. That was so many years back before he finally won the Presidential seat in 2000. I am very certain that a lot of hard work, discipline, self-denial, total commitment and dedication, seriousness, concentration and focus, intelligence, sacrifice, humility, prayers, and financial resources went into realizing that vision.

Vision does not need verbal communication; it needs action to communicate it. Provide enough intrinsic energy, intellectual and financial resources to fuel your vision. I was not surprised to have heard this powerful and unequivocal statement, "A vision without provision leads to the revision of the vision" from Rev. Eastwood Anaba. Strict adherence to his statement puts you on the success way to the top. Provide enough provision to sustain your vision. Visions can be permanent or temporal.

PERMANENT VISIONS

Your permanent vision(s) can be one or two or three depending on your mental capacity and ability and the level of influence and power you want to carry in time and eternity. A Medical Officer who doubles as a Lecturer and at the same time, an Army Officer is an example. There are several examples.

TEMPORAL VISIONS

Temporal visions however, are many short term visions supporting your permanent visions. They are well calculated visions that are in consistent agreement with your main ultimate permanent vision. Your success depends on the way you work towards the accomplishments of your temporal visions. If for instance, your main vision is to become an established Politician, then your temporal visions will include actively involving yourself in students' activism (politics) at all levels on your academic ladder. Each academic level students' leadership is a temporal vision or ambition. This prepares and ushers you into your ultimate vision.

- **HOW VISIONS BECOME GOALS**

Set goals from your vision, break the rules and dare to be different. You're exactly what the world has been waiting for. Start your engines and say to yourself "Here I come world", and don't get intimidated by the traffic but keep your eyes fixed on your goals and the destination. Go the extra mile until there are no more miles to be covered. It wouldn't be easy, but it'll eventually be worth it.

A goal is a vision narrowed and broken down into achievable form with this acronym in mind; SMART. Your goal must be specific, measurable, achievable, and realistic and time bound. This is the stage where you clearly state the time range you want to accomplish your goal. Your goal rejuvenates your spirit man and rekindles the enthusiasm and emotions with which your entire being accepted the thought the very day it was nursed. A vision that is not transformed into a goal is just a paper work. Your goals give you a sense of direction, focus, and urgency and an urge to remain serious. The challenges, troubles, disappointments, life's ups and downs will definitely come as far as you are alive, but never get discouraged, distraught, disheartened or lose focus on your goals and ideals because those who succeeded never had it on silver platter. Let any negative life experience be a motivating factor and never a discouraging factor.

Everyone has got dreams, even the foetus under conception dreams to one day behold the lovely face of the woman whose womb has granted it such warmth and security. Whatever dreams we have are actually possible when we set goals from them. They can be achieved. All that is required is a little focus, a pint of self-denial, constant practice and an unwavering self-confidence. We sometimes start off very well, but just when the going begins to get tough, we throw in the towel - forgetting that the darkest part of the night is succeeded by the rising sun. Live your dreams, one day they shall hatch and you shall see them grow.

TYPES OF GOALS

There are three types of goals. Set immediate, intermediate and long-range goals. **Immediate goals** are closest, nearest or next in order. These goals are tasks or objectives that are accomplished in a day or two. It has a period from one to ninety days. However, you can further break it down this way: (1 to 30 days); (31 to 60 days); (61 to 90 days). Usually, these tasks are accomplished quickly without a great deal of energy and planning. Intermediate goals are medium term goals that require multiple strategic steps and planning for their completion. **Intermediate goals** can only be accomplished after you have successfully accomplished immediate goals in succession. **Intermediate goals** require more unfailing and uninterrupted direction in your life. They may span from ninety days to three years. You can break it down this way: (90 days to 6 months); (6 months to 1 year); (1 to 3 years). The long-range goals further take the future into consideration. They are connected to your life's work, career, and professional objectives. **Long-range goals** need thorough planning, preparation and execution. They are consistent with and support your life vision or purpose. Your long-range goals are established on consistent and continuous accomplishment of your immediate and intermediate goals. Their accomplishment require from three years to a lifetime: (3 to 5 years); (5 to 10); (10 years to a lifetime).

SIX QUALITIES YOUR GOALS MUST HAVE

Every goal must be written, committed to, and shared. Writing down your goals makes you crystallize what exactly you want to accomplish. Summarize each goal in only one or two short, simple, and concise sentence(s). Read, memorize and recite it daily. This makes you think about it, remember it, and act on it. Make a binding covenant with yourself that nothing and no one will stop you from attaining your goal. Give your time, efforts, expertise, resources, and anything less necessary to accomplish your goal. Share your goal with likeminded people. Be however; smart never to share your goals, dreams and aspirations with dream killers and destroyers. Very often, dream killers are family members and close associates or friends. Share it with people who can objectively criticize you, assist and encourage you, not those who will become jealous or envious.

Every goal must be realistic and attainable. Most enthusiastic young professionals have failed because they set improper goals which were unrealistic. No goal is impossible, but it may be unrealistic at your particular state in development or at a given time. Imagine I have set a goal to buy and own an English Premier League Club in the next five years. I will be deceiving myself. Make sure that your goals are realistic and attainable for you, based on where you are right now.

Every goal must be flexible and reflect change. Your goal is a statement and projection of your vision. However, along the line as you progress into the future, external influences and circumstances beyond your control may appear. These are potential things that can prevent you from attaining your goal. When this interference occurs, don't be discouraged or abandon your goal. You must quickly re-strategize and make necessary changes and modifications to your goal, or to the manner of pursuing it. That will counterbalance the condition or circumstance that is hindering your progress.

Every goal must be set in advance. Your goal is a destination, the desired outcome of your endeavours. If it is not set in advance, neither strategic plans nor effective steps be employed to attain it. When your goals are set in advance, you give yourself a particular orientation to your life and this brings attention to your energy and thoughts.

Every goal must be concrete and measurable. Let your goal be as clear as crystal and as white as snow. Use all your senses in this case: sight your goal, feel it, smell it, taste it, and sound it. See your goal in its size, colour, location, movement, and other characteristics possible. Your goal must be measurable to determine its dimensions. With a measurable goal, you can set standard by analysing and estimating its completion. If it is not measurable, it is very difficult to project when you will attain it, how far you have to go, or how much effort it will take. Setting a goal that is not measurable is like sparking a car to an undetermined destination. You will `ride and ride, but will never get there.

Your goal must be extended to cover certain time periods. You must set specific time intervals for the accomplishment of your goals. This helps you to harness all your intrinsic energy and power in accomplishing your goal. The time period should be realistic in light of your particular level of skill, the time and the resources you have available, time constraints of the goal itself, and the standards of past performances by yourself and others. Putting a time component into your goal gives you the means by which to examine your performance and project your completion. If, based on monitoring your own performance, the projected time for completion is unreasonable or unacceptable; you can increase your efforts, modify your timetable, or even alter your goal accordingly.

CATEGORIES OF GOALS

These are ***goals in continuity to progression and goals in opposition to progression.*** Goals in continuity to progression are reasonable estimations of your current state and your preparedness to improve. These goals lead you into your desired future. For instance, if you have a goal like this: "I would be a professional Journalist", then you must have mini goals; Goal #1 - Attend basic school and complete with best result. Goal #2 - Get admitted to a senior high school of choice and complete with best result. Goal #3 Get admitted to a journalism school of choice and graduate with best result. Goal #4 - Do your professional career attachment with a reputable media house. Goal #5 - Successfully secure a job in the best media group of choice.

Goals in opposition to progression are goals representing a complete change in your current condition or situation. They may represent an abrupt or sudden change in the direction of your life. For example, a goal in opposition would be; after drinking a bottle of beer a day for the past ten years, you decide today to stop drinking immediately. Your decision to quit drinking immediately is a goal in opposition because it represents a complete change in what you have been doing for the last ten years. It is harder to accomplish but if that accomplishment is made, it ensures progression of your life.

ACHIEVING YOUR GOALS

Set a goal for one year. Determine what needs to be done to accomplish your goal. Set monthly goals that will lead you to your full-year goal. Determine what needs to be done to accomplish each monthly goal. Set weekly goals for the first month. Determine what must be done to accomplish the goals of the first week of the first month. Set daily goals for the first week of the first month. Determine what actions must be performed each day to accomplish your daily goals. Keep a record of your achievements. Learn from past failures but don't allow them to slow your progress. Avoid time wasting. Repeat this procedure without fail. Stick to your goal until it is accomplished.

- **HOW GOALS BECOME PLANS**

You were born to win, but to be a winner; you must plan to win, prepare to win and expect to win. - Zig Ziglar

Many people nurtured the thoughts, felt the uncontrollable emotions, and wrote down their visions and goals but failed to plan for the proper execution of their goals. If you fail to plan, you plan to fail. Nothing good comes on a silver platter. It is actually free to think and imagine big things in life. Every ordinary person thinks and imagines. But what makes those thoughts become a reality is by strategic planning and timely execution of the plans. You can't be a winner if you are not a strategic planner. The day you start to fail planning your life that is the day you start failing in life. Every winner is a planner. However, not every planner is a winner. Beyond the planning, there must be action to ensure the victory. Plan your goals by planning your activities. Planning is simply the preparations or the activities and measures put in place to ensure that an intended target or goal is met. Preparation is powerful in ensuring victory. If you want to achieve your goals, you must plan in advance.

Planning in advance makes you brood over your strategies for an appreciable period of time. It makes you to evaluate your chances, assess your strengths and weaknesses, and weigh the time duration within which the goal is to be achieved. Just as there are immediate, intermediate and long-range goals, in the same vein, there are corresponding immediate, intermediate and long-range plans. If you operate in this reality; you will be ahead of time and your contemporaries as your plans will stretch farther into the future. If your plans stretch into the future, you have ample time to deploy and employ all relevant forces needed for the timely execution of your plans.

The most important element in attaining your goals is the formation and execution of definite, practical plans which work. Constantly monitor the productiveness of your plan. Evaluate the productiveness of your plan on a daily basis. If your plan works, double your efforts for even greater results. Do not waste time on a plan that does not work. If your plan does not lead you on a continuous, step-by-step journey towards your goals, replace it with a new plan. If the new plan does not work either, replace it with still another plan. Continue monitoring and evaluating your plan until you find one that works for you. Give each plan sufficient time interval to produce expected results.

THE SUCCESS PLAN

Purchase a book and make it your daily planner. Write your vision, goals, and target dates in your planner. List the actions necessary to accomplish your goals, and when they must be performed. Write out a brief, but complete narrative statement of how you intend to achieve your goals. Revise, study, digest, and memorize your success plan statement. Start right away doing the most important things first, and then proceeding to less important ones. Develop a daily timetable showing all actions to be performed and the dates they must be done. Plan all actions that must be performed each day. Monitor your efforts closely and evaluate your results.

- **HOW PLANS BECOME ACTIONS**

Action is the operating procedure by which your thoughts and emotions become the things and experiences of your life. "The only place where success comes before work is in the dictionary." said, Vidal Sassoon. Joel Barker also advised that, "Vision without action is merely a dream. Action without vision just passes the time. Vision with action can change the world". Just as sacrifice and self-denial makes the hen to physically lose weight while sitting on her eggs due to decreased feeding, so you must also deny yourself the pleasures of the world by working your plans. One thing you must not forget is that time waits for no man. Whether you act or not, time will continue to make an unrepeatable and irreplaceable progress. Believe it or not; as the days go by, your life span shortens, your energy reduces, your unaccomplished goals stare at you, health problems set in, but your burden and expenditure increase exponentially.

With this in mind, don't waste time. Start acting now and stick to all your plans. After planning your work, work your plans. When the hen starts sitting on her eggs, she minimizes movement. That is a sign of discipline. Discipline yourself and restrict your movements. You need more time to work, not more time to move about. There is power in your actions whether intentionally or unintentionally. Your actions bring results. You can get expected or good results only when you act your plans. Interestingly, you get best results when you have worked hard and gone beyond the limit. Best results come to the extra mile goers. The extra mile goers don't go to sleep whilst there is work to be done, they don't hover and loiter about either. They internalize and emotionalize their vision and plans and so they constantly execute their plans to the latter.

Surround yourself with those who will bring out the best in you, not the stress in you. Associate yourself with people who will motivate, encourage and challenge you to work harder and go the extra mile. When you mingle with the extra mile goers, you become an extra mile goer. All that is written in this book and in all other instruments of enlightenment are absolutely worthless unless you put these ideas and principles into action. James 1:22 says "Do not merely listen to the word, and so deceive yourselves, Do what it says". There are many young professionals who are only competing for space at the top in their mouth. They are lazy and are deceiving themselves that they will reach the top. Don't be one of them! Remember the top is not for chickens but eagles. The only way to the top is by acting your plans. The top dwellers are the actors and actors are the top dwellers. There is no other alternative. Most politicians who win elections are people who have spent enough time, energy, resources, et cetera working on the ground. Business moguls, successful musicians, excellent sports men, influential men of God, great authors and motivational speakers, professional journalists, celebrities, rulers of the world economy and governance, great educationists, respectable doctors and lawyers, et cetera all have a secret. And the secret is they work harder than expected.

The reason some people are making it big and others are struggling is that God has placed treasure in hard work. Irrespective of your faith, believe, race, educational status, if you work hard, you will find that treasure.

God is the Father for all so He rewards hard work. Many Christians are poor because they think God will put money in their pockets when they don't work for it. Note this: God will not do by miracle what you are supposed to do as your responsibility. Your vision will never be realized if you don't act your plans. Your goal will only materialize after you have strategically acted your plans. Many people believe work is a means to make a living but I believe work is a means to live your making. When you work as a means to live your making, you naturally appear happy and joyous within. Any work at all you find yourself doing, you do it with all your heart and this develops your inner gifts quickly and timely. On the other hand, if you work as a means of making a living, you may expose yourself to and do works that you don't love. You do those works simply because of the income it brings you. In this case, you may not have inner joy and satisfaction even though you are working. As a student, you must study very hard if only you want to obtain best results.

You must prepare for situation resolution. Write down the situation. Analyze the situation. List all the alternative solutions. Evaluate all possible solutions. Determine if your solution benefits others. Picture the consequences. Get advice, but make the decision your own. Stick to your decision. Instantly put your decision into action.

- **HOW ACTIONS BECOME RESULTS**

Results are unavoidable in life. Results will always come at the end of every step and decision you make in life. Even if you don't make any decision or you haven't made any move about your situation, there will still be result. As to whether the result is desirable or undesirable, it largely depends on the planning and the actions that went into the execution of the decision in actualizing and fulfilling your goals. Whether you take actions or not, there will be results. There are enormous results that have occurred in the lives of some people who believed they never deserved that outcome.

My question is "If you think you don't deserve that outcome, who then deserves it?" It is because you haven't made the necessary strategic plans and fully implemented your plans with enthusiasm and action, that is why, you get the undesired results.

If your topmost prayer point is God should make you rich, yet you don't have financial wisdom on how to make money, how to keep money, and how to grow (multiply) money, you will continue to remain poor, grow poorer, and eventually die the poorest. There may be moments and times when you will systematically and effortfully apply all the needed principles, yet you will amazingly get the undesired result. It may be painful but never regret it. Never lose hope, faith and trust in God. Your right time will definitely come as far as you remain committed to God and your vision. John Aughey advised "God brings men into deeper waters not to drown them but to cleanse them." God may be cleansing you for a higher task you have no idea of. But in order to qualify for such task and make the awesome impact He requires of you, you must go through this preparation and get yourself adequately ready for that task. Your failure to go through the preparatory stage means you have disqualified yourself for the task.

This is how our thoughts become results.

In making or transforming your thoughts into results, you need role players in your life. Check it out in the next chapter.

YOUR DIVINE HELPERS

Your Divine Helpers are people who have identified some good qualities and potentials in you and have decided to assist or bless you so you could unleash those potentials and qualities in you to the fullest for the benefit of humanity and for the glory of God to be revealed. Our destinies are somewhat tied with our divine helpers and so we cannot do away with our divine helpers. Anyone who assists you in time of adversity, sadness, loneliness and rejection is your divine helper. Your divine helper can be anyone at all around you. From the definition above, we can learn a lot of lessons. Taking a closer look at the definition, the following have been revealed:

- Your divine helpers identify you first.

- They have seen good qualities and potentials (star) in you.
- They have decided to assist or bless you so you could unleash your potentials and qualities to the fullest.
- Their decision is to benefit mankind.
- Their decision is to reveal God's glory.

After Jesus was born in Bethlehem in Judea, during the time of King Herod, Magi from the east came to Jerusalem. And asked, "Where is the one who has been born King of the Jews? We saw his star in the east and we have come to worship him" (Matthew 2:1-2)

On coming to the house, they saw the child with his mother Mary, and they bowed down and worshipped him. Then they opened their treasures and presented him with gifts of gold and of incense and myrrh. (Matthew 2:11)

The above scriptures further reveal the mystery in the points listed earlier. The wise men saw the star and were able to identify it as the star of the Messiah. They saw the qualities and the potentials in the Messiah and so they called him King of the Jews. It was a collective human decision by the Magi to come and bless Jesus with gifts. Their visit and blessing was to spiritually unleash the potentials and qualities of Jesus to the fullest. This is evident when they went to King Herod and proclaimed to him that a new King was born and that they were there to worship him. Bible theologians will make you understand that the treasures and gold presented to Jesus was more than enough to make his parents very wealthy. Their presentation has benefited Jesus' immediate family and the entire human race. The glory of God was as well revealed.

The scripture has further revealed that it was the Magi that first identified the new born King and not the child's parent or the child himself.

However, the child's parent received the gifts on behalf of the child because they had spiritual discernment to identify them as divine helpers.

On the journey to achieving personal development, prosperity, success and destiny fulfilment, God has positioned divine helpers at every stage and moment of your life. It is your duty to identify and efficiently utilize them to fulfil the divine purposes of God concerning your life. Your ability to have the discerning spirit to identify them is one of the major hurdles to cross. The identification process is usually not difficult because these divine helpers are naturally bonded and attracted to you since they have a divine role to play in your life. However, sometimes they may come to you in disguise and so you are likely to miss them. After the identification stage is successfully over, the greatest challenge is how to keep and fully utilize these important people in your life. I must confess that these are the most important people in your life apart from your Creator and family.

HOW TO IDENTIFY AND KNOW YOUR DIVINE HELPERS

You need prayer and spiritual discernment to identify your divine helpers as they come your way. The tree analogy used by someone best explains the kind of people we encounter and interact with on daily basis and in our entire stay on earth. Come to think of people in my own life, be it friends, family, acquaintances, employees, co-workers, whomever...They are all placed inside and perfectly fit into this simple tree test. It goes like this:

THE LEAF PEOPLE

Some people come into your life and they are like leaves on a tree. They are only there for a season. You can't depend on them or count on them because they are weak and only there to give you shade. Like leaves, they are there to take what they need and as soon as it gets cold or a wind blows in your life they are gone. You can't be angry at them, it's just who they are.

THE BRANCH PEOPLE

There are some people who come into your life and they are like branches on a tree. They are stronger than leaves, but you have to be careful with them. They will stick around through most seasons, but if you go through a storm or two in your life, it's possible that you could lose them.

Most times they break away when it's tough. Although they are stronger than leaves, you have to test them out before you run out there and put all your weight on them. In most cases they can't handle too much weight. But again, you can't be mad with them, it's just who they are.

THE ROOT PEOPLE

If you can find some people in your life who are like the roots of a tree then you have found a special thing. Like the roots of a tree, they are hard to find because they are not trying to be seen. Their only job is to hold you up and help you live a strong and healthy life. If you thrive, they are happy. They stay low key and don't let the world know that they are there. And if you go through an awful storm they will hold you up. Their job is to hold you up, come what may, and to nourish you, feed you and water you. These are your true divine helpers. Thank God for the roots underneath your tree of life. Just as a tree has many limbs and many leaves, there are few roots. Look at your own life. How many leaves, branches and roots do you have? What are you in other people's lives?

Hosea 12:13 tells us that "…by a prophet the LORD brought Israel out of Egypt, and by a prophet was he preserved." Notice, He didn't say, "…by an angel," but "…by a prophet." God preserves or establishes His people through His servants; His chosen and anointed ministers in any field of calling. He equips them and sends them to those He wants to bless. Ephesians 4:11-12 says, "And he gave some, apostles; and some, prophets; and some, evangelists; and some, pastors and teachers; for the perfecting of the saints, for the work of the ministry, for the edifying of the body of Christ." God has blessed someone because of you so take advantage and get blessed because you are ordained for that blessing.

Your divine helpers serve as signpost that directs your navigation through the journey of this murky world. Life is a very big rough and smooth road full of signposts pointing to various destinations. Passengers or travellers on this road must be extremely careful and vigilant in order to reach their desired destination. Drivers and sailors are directed by road signs and major landmarks respectively so they could reach their destinations safely, so we as humans are also directed by the people planted by God for a fulfilled life.

It is worth noting that you meet these personalities from the day of birth through to your day of death. By their deeds, you will know them with discernment. Some can spend their entire life blessing and assisting you to prosper whilst others will only spend some few days, or months, or years with you. But whatever the case may be, they always appear in the most critical moment or stage of your life.

HOW TO KEEP AND EFFECTIVELY UTILIZE YOUR DIVINE HELPERS

After successfully identifying and knowing your divine helpers, you have a role to play in keeping them and here they are:

- It is your duty to keep them
- It is your duty to fully utilize them

Whether they will stay and accomplish the purpose for which they were brought into your life or leave you without accomplishing why they came into your life depends on a number of divine principles. Your readiness and ability to obey and observe these golden principles is what does the magic.

Just like how continuously watering the tree or plant with salty water will cause the tree to die prematurely because of the disturbances the salty water causes to the roots, so it is with our divine helpers. If you want the plant or tree to grow bigger and bear good and multiple fruits, you need to use good water in watering it, you need to prune it and remove the unwanted weeds growing around it. If you want to keep and fully utilize your divine helpers, you need to observe and obey the divine principles that come with their existence in your life. I will take my time to take you through these powerful principles one after the other.

1. RESPECTFULNESS AND HUMILITY

Respect costs you nothing yet it buys everything. The best currency in the world is respect. It buys every valuable commodity in all nations because it has and will always continue to remain an international currency. The secret to personal success is to possess the respect currency. Respect is one of the few assets that bring us fame, wealth, power and influence. Humility is synonymous to respectfulness. However, humility shows how we have totally surrendered ourselves to other people or God. Obedience is embedded in humility because humility will cause you to obey all instructions and directives. Every humble individual is an obedient person. That is why you need to be respectful and humble in order to receive from all manner of people. I have observed that our divine helpers at any point in life are mostly older than us. In some cases, the reverse may also be true.

The first thing our divine helpers look out for in us is to see how we respect others and our level of humility. It is very true that first impressions count but remember it will never last longer if you are faking it all. You will miss your divine helpers if you are arrogant and disobedient. This negative character will repel your helpers. This is because the negative character mostly covers your star from being identified and so nobody sees anything good in you. Sometimes, your helpers may get magnetized to you with the sole aim of fulfilling their role in your life, but your arrogance and disobedience may repel them. In order to receive all the blessings or assistance from your divine helpers, you need to respect and obey them irrespective of age, culture or race. The law of receiving states that "you cannot receive anything good from someone you do not respect and obey". Without respect and humility, you are not in any better position to receive anything good from your divine helpers.

THE DEEPER REVELATION IN THE ELIJAH AND ELISHA ENCOUNTER

*Elijah took his cloak, rolled it up and struck the water with it. The water divided to the right and to the left, and the two of them crossed over on dry ground. When they had crossed, Elijah said to Elisha, **"Tell me, what can I do for you before I am taken from you?"** "Let me inherit a double portion of your spirit" Elisha replied. "You have asked a difficult thing," Elijah said, **"yet if you see me when I am taken from you, it will be yours – otherwise not."** As they were walking along and talking together, suddenly a chariot of fire and horses of fire appeared and separated the two of them, and Elijah went up to heaven in a whirlwind. Elisha saw this and cried out, "My father! My father! The chariots and horsemen of Israel!" And Elisha saw him no more. Then he took hold of his own clothes and tore them apart. He picked up the cloak that had fallen from Elijah and went back and stood on the bank of the Jordan.* (2nd Kings 2:8-13)

This is a common story known by most Christians. Before the spiritual impartation took place in the scriptures above, something intriguing happened. There was a free will gift which Elijah wanted to give Elisha based on what he, the receiver (Elisha), so desired but amazingly, there was a condition attached to it. Until the condition was fully satisfied, Elisha would not have received that which he wanted. It was a gift that did not require money or anything precious in exchange, yet many Christians of our generation would have missed it. The condition as highlighted above can only be satisfied by a respectful humble obedient child whose eyes are gazed on Elijah with a hundred percent concentration or focus. The scripture further reveals that "they were walking along and talking together". That was a distractive moment and a moment where you can easily lose focus if you are not disciplined and obedient. This is because as you walk, you need to look forward so you do not hit your foot against any stone and hurt yourself. I am convinced that they were not journeying on a tarred road. If it were a tarred road, there would be no stone to hit your foot against. In an attempt not to hurt your foot, your total focus cannot be on the giver (Elijah) because you need to look forward as well.

At the same time, we are made to understand that they were conversing. An enjoyable conversation like the one between Elijah and Elisha needed the attention of both but most importantly, Elisha. I believe Elisha was very attentive in the conversation with his master because he did not want to miss the last words of his master at that crucial moment. It will be suicidal if he should miss his master's last words as a result of his inattentiveness. Attention can only be achieved with a concentrated mind. Again, this was another issue that took part of Elisha's concentration away from gazing directly on his master. Shockingly, in this distractive moment, the scripture records that "suddenly a chariot of fire and horses of fire appeared and separated the two of them, and Elijah went up to heaven in a whirlwind." As I said earlier, many Christians of our time would have missed it because the whole rapture happened within a blink of an eye in a distractive moment. Yet Elisha saw it and cried out. He really deserved the double portion of the anointing he received because he was smart in fulfilling the condition. The whole condition was to see his master been raptured and this he perfectly did. The second coming of our Lord Jesus Christ will not be different from this scenario. We must beware as Christians; else most Christians will miss it.

Most often than not, our divine helpers give us the opportunity to choose what we want. But whatever choice you make, there is a condition attached to it. It takes respect and humility to satisfy these conditions. These conditions appear so simple and doable yet they are not easily satisfiable. Most Christians cannot satisfy these conditions because they lack respect for the gift offered them and as well lack discipline and humility. Many destinies have not been touched by their divine hands, not because the divine hands are not there, but, because owners of those destinies have not been able to satisfy the conditions given by their divine helpers. Any condition such as sexual favours, pilfering and corrupt practices should tell you that you are not dealing with your divine helper, but "hell helper". Divine helpers strengthen your relationship with God. One of the inevitable ways to the top is to be respectful and humble.

THE DEEPER REVELATION IN JESUS' ENCOUNTER WITH THE SERVANTS AT THE WEDDING CEREMONY

On the third day a wedding took place at Cana in Galilee. Jesus' mother was there, and Jesus and his disciples had also been invited to the wedding. When the wine was gone, Jesus' mother said to him "They have no more wine". "Dear woman, why do you involve me?" Jesus replied, "My time has not yet come". His mother said to the servants, ***"Do whatever he tells you".*** *Nearby stood six stone jars, the kind used by the Jews for ceremonial washing, each holding from twenty to thirty gallons.* ***Jesus said to the servants "Fill***

the jars with water"; *so they filled them to the brim.* ***Then he told them, "Now draw some out and take it to the master of the banquet" They did so.*** *(John 2:1-8) (NIV)*

The first miracle of Jesus in the Bible was performed after a condition was satisfied by the servants. Many believers do not know this truth. After Mary approached Jesus and discussed the matter with him, she actually came back to the servants and gave them a command even though she heard nothing encouraging from the conversation she had with Jesus. She said, "Do whatever he tells you". In other words, she told them, "obey what he tells you to do without questioning". This means that the solution to the problem was directly dependent on the obedience or otherwise of the servants. So what was needed to satisfy the condition was neither money nor anything physically valuable or precious, but the attitude of respectfulness and obedience to the orders of Jesus. If they had disobeyed Jesus' orders, no miracle would have happened.

It is worth noting that the couple was not those to satisfy the condition even though they were the direct beneficiaries of the miracle. It was their servants. Sometimes we receive our breakthroughs or promotions or get a way to the top not because we as individuals have satisfied the conditions given by our divine helpers, but someone connected to our life has satisfied the conditions in our stead. And this is exactly what happened in this case. That is why you must respect and humble yourself to people around you and most importantly, the least ones because you have no idea which of them will satisfy a particular condition in your stead for your promotion. The way to the top is very smooth for strategic people but very rough for those who have failed to strategize.

Jesus gave two commands and these commands were very strange and meaningless to the servants, yet they obeyed. In a moment of such, you do not try to show your intelligence and professionalism else you will miss the target and the intended results will not be achieved. These servants I believe were technical men and specialists in wine production and they knew exactly the processes and steps wine production goes through. If they knew nothing about wine production and how it is served, Mary would not have contacted them. Anytime you attend a wedding ceremony, you will observe that the caterers are the same as the food servers and those who serve the drinks are people who have knowledge on distilleries. Jesus did not use any principles employed in wine production. He used his own self-employed principles which made no sense to these professional wine producers. The condition given them was to obey whatever Jesus said but not in the full glare of total flooring of the very principles governing their profession and disregard for it with strange and meaningless commands. Moreover, they knew that Jesus was not a specialist in that field more than them. It is interesting to know that Jesus had not done any miracle to his credit then for the servants to have confidence and faith him. It is amazing none of them questioned Jesus about his strange directives.

However, they had faith and confidence in him. In fact, these servants had a very great and unshakable faith looking at the circumstances surrounding the incident. It is evident that they did not know what was happening, yet they were carrying out orders. This is total humility and obedience. If we modern day Christians can follow the example of these humble servants, no Christian will miss his divine promoter on the journey of success and personal development. I pray that even as you read this book, you will receive spiritual discernment to identify your divine promoters and the spirit of respectfulness and humility to keep and utilize them in your life.

There is another important lesson we can add to the lessons learnt already in the above scripture. That is:

- The condition giver was Mary
- The blessing/gift/miracle receiver was the couple
- The condition satisfiers were the servants
- The miracle/blessing giver was Jesus

There are times in life where you need three different categories of role players in order for a divine assignment to be fulfilled in your life. What you need to do as the beneficiary is to identify these candidates and utilize them.

ALIKO DANGOTE AND BENSON IDAHOSA ENCOUNTER

As I was researching on the internet one day, I came across this piece and it's worth sharing in this book.

If you will only let me help you, if you will only obey, then I will make you rich. (Isaiah 1:19)

Aliko Dangote was born into a wealthy home in Kano. He got his first degree in Cairo, Egypt. He had always loved trading, and reports say he hawked sweets even as a primary school child, even though his family was wealthy. Dangote is really a very humble person even by the confessions of people who have interacted with him. But Dangote is not the only hardworking Nigerian. He is not the only humble person around. He is probably not the most business savvy in Africa. But he is certainly the richest Blackman in the world. As at 2015, his companies employ over 11, 000 people directly – not to mention, distributors, contractors and other vendors who depend on his businesses to thrive. Dangote is a blessing to humanity.

There is no family in Nigeria today that does not have a Dangote product in their home. If it is not sugar, then it is salt or the house you are living in was built with Dangote Cement. Everyone has something to do with his business, so like Job he earns a little off everyone and that is the way to get wealthy. In 2015, Dangote was ranked the 23rd richest person in the world and is said to be the second most powerful African alive. The question is how did Dangote attain such a height? Yes, you can't take away his hard work and business acumen, but that is only the starting point. The answer will not be found in the Forbes Magazine or on Wikipedia. The answer is in the verse of scripture quoted above: If you are willing and obedient you will eat the good of the land.

Sometime in the early 1990s Dangote had an encounter with a divine helper that set his foot on the path of destiny. Archbishop Benson Idahosa of blessed memory had some guests who needed to travel back urgently from Benin to Lagos to catch up their flight to the US. Unfortunately, by the time the Archbishop took his guests to the airport, they were told that the last flight for the day was overbooked and not a single seat was available. As a matter of fact, the passengers have boarded and were about to take off. Idahosa asked for the plane to be delayed a few minutes and walked to the tarmac where he was allowed to address the passengers. He pleaded with them about the desperate situation of his guests and asked that two persons should donate their seats for his guests to get to Lagos.

Almost, everyone in that plane was a Christian. Not one of them batted an eyelid. Some pretended to be asleep, some pretended to be praying and the Man of God stood waiting. From the back of the plane, a young man asked the person sitting next to him to get up and together they vacated their seat for the American visitors. Idahosa stopped him in the aisle of the plane and asked, "Young man, what is your name and what do you do?" "My name is Dangote, Aliko Dangote and this is my assistant. I am a trader, a businessman." It was there and then, that Bishop Idahosa prophesied to him that "the world will get up for you". He prayed that God should take his business beyond Africa and bless him beyond measure. Today God has answered that prayer. God destined that blessing for someone seated in that plane that evening. But there was a condition attached to it. Isaiah 1:19 says If you will only let me help you, if you will only obey, then I will make you rich. Dangote's wealth today was not meant for a Christian businessman who was too proud, too fixated in his mind, but to a humble spirited man. The question is if you were there on that plane, would you have taken the blessing?

Life is too small to feel bigger or better than anybody. "We're all naked to death" says Steve Jobs. Nothing can save us from it. Many destinies have not been fulfilled because our generation is full of arrogant and disobedient children.

2. MAINTAIN YOUR INTEGRITY AND CREDIBILITY

The foundation stones for a balanced success are honesty, character, integrity, faith, love and loyalty. - Zig Ziglar

Integrity is a state where your deeds and nature are in consistent perpetual agreement with your words. It is important to always maintain your integrity. Never allow your integrity to be questioned; else everyone would take you for granted. It is an undeniable fact that integrity is a state or level everyone must yearn to reach in life. Reaching the status where your deeds and nature are in consistent perpetual agreement with your words is not achieved overnight and it is not as easy as we see it. In other words, doing exactly what you preach. However, some individuals have managed to reach that level. But maintaining their integrity at the level they have reached in life is the greatest challenge. Integrity is very expensive; don't expect it from cheap people. Anyone whose integrity remains intact is a man worth celebrating and emulating by his generation and the generations after him.

Is there any role your integrity and credibility must play in keeping your divine helpers with you? The answer is Yes…God in his own wisdom and might has positioned these divine helpers in our lives so that the very moment we encounter them, we will have our breakthrough immediately or we will not be too far from our breakthroughs. However, this will not happen if your divine helper doubts your credibility and integrity. If you give an opportunity to your divine helpers to doubt your credibility and integrity in a situation where they least expected it, their trust, faith and hope in you may dwindle and this will quench the enthusiasm and zeal with which they were prepared to help you go far in life. No one will be prepared to support or bless you with their financial and intellectual resources for you to succeed unless you have given them enough reasons that you are the best candidate for that support or blessing.

One thing you must not forget is that your divine helpers mostly observe you from afar without your notice. They have made a complete positive mental impression about you before letting you know of their intentions for your life. Your responsibility is to maintain that impression which they made earlier about you and try to even improve upon it. Anything substandard to the earlier impression will result in disappointment and regret. Remember that one of their core mandates is to bless and project you for community or societal or national or international recognition so you will in turn bless other people to prosper. Someone's destiny directly depends on you because you are their divine helper. You must be truthful and honest to your divine helpers in all matters and circumstances. That is what they need from you and you must be ready to deliver it to them. Anything contrary to that request is suicidal for your progress.

Interestingly, they never openly request for it yet they expect it and you need to give them.

Do not be deceived for God is not mocked. A man reaps what he sows. (Galatians 6:7)

If you cannot bless others, especially, the vulnerable ones who need your assistance most with your resources due to your selfish ambitions and corrupt practices, why should your divine helper support you to succeed in life?

3. PRAYER

"If you believe, you will receive whatever you ask for in prayer"
Matthew 21: 22

Prayer to me is an intimate encounter, fellowship and communion between man and divinity. Anytime we vehemently pray, heavens open and God communes with our spirit. There is more to prayer than just a communication between two spirits as people may have believed. As a Christian, anytime all your friends, colleagues, business partners complain of your scarcity in their midst, know that you are actually spending more quality time in the presence of Elohim and that is a sign of spiritual growth and maturity. Anytime you spend more time with friends, colleagues, business partners, it is a sign of spiritual declination.

Prayer increases your level of discernment and makes you know your divine helpers. There are times when fervent prayer quickens the arrival and the activities of divine helpers. John Wesley once said, "It appears as if God will do nothing for man except he prays." Pray for your divine helpers on daily basis for God to bless and increase them.

The eagle changes the battle ground when it picks up snake into the sky and releases it into the air. The eagle will never fight snake on the ground. The snake has no stamina, no power and no balance in the air. It is useless, weak and vulnerable unlike on the ground where it is powerful, wise and deadly. Take your fight into the spiritual realm by praying and when you are in the spiritual realm, God takes over your battles. Don't fight your enemies in their comfort zones, change the battle grounds and let God take charge through your earnest prayer. You'll be assured of clean and sound victory. Have faith in your prayers because God will never answer doubtful prayers. Pray without ceasing. Saying you can't pray because you have committed too many sins, is like saying you can't shower because you're too dirty. Your knees are your strongest assets. Anyone who kneels before God stands before men. He that sweats in prayer never bleeds in battle. The kneeler is invariably the tallest.

As a child, anytime I was trekking with my dad to a nearby village in the night and I heard unfamiliar sounds in the surrounding bushes which appeared to me as life-threatening moments, I quickly clung unto my dad and held him tightly such that I don't miss and lose him. That moment was not the time to run away from my dad but to cling unto him tightly. I may be running into danger and become helpless.

In life, in perceived life-threatening, challenging and difficult moments, cling unto God and hold him tightly as never before. That is not the moment to run away from God and seek refuge elsewhere. There are some problems that seem not to have solution until you go on your knees in vehement prayer. Cultivate and maintain the habit of prayer because sometimes it is only prayer that can sustain you in the storm. Continue to pray for your helpers. Pray for them like how you pray for yourself because they have the mandate of heaven to bless and increase your life.

4. COMMUNICATION AND GRATITUDE

The joy, happiness and peace in every relationship or engagement ride on the back of constant effective communication. There must always be an effective constant communication between you and your divine helpers.

Communication is one of the things that bond you to your divine helpers such that separation becomes extremely difficult. Effective and productive communication increases the duration your divine helpers spend in your life. Communication is in several forms; phone calls, text messages, emails, and home visits. Use them in different ways to convey your messages to them in appealing presentable acceptable manner. Be in touch with them. Let them be aware that you appreciate their support and the only perfect way to do that is through effective communication. It makes you know their routine schedules and sometimes their challenges as they may share them with you. Show concern and offer assistance if you are in the capacity to do so. For someone to share his/her challenges with you, it is a sign that he/she has some level of trust and believes in you. It does not just happen, it comes when communication becomes constant and effective. This is what develops the trust.

Naturally, we feel happy and special when friends and loved ones call us on phone or send us text messages just wanting to know how we are faring. It is a universal principle and it works across every culture and race. Do same for the divine role players in your life at acceptable time intervals. At least once a week will do the magic. Do not wait and only call them when you have troubles or financial challenges. You may infuriate them and may not receive their full support because they are not your bank where you only go for withdrawals.

A break in communication means a break in engagement or relationship. Do not create a communication barrier because it will adversely affect you especially in situations where your helpers have not fully accomplished their divine task in your life. Communication gap is suicidal and very toxic to progress, success and fulfilment just as ammonia is toxic to neurons.

Good communication is the single most effective and efficient tool of successful and excellent people; leaders and their subjects, husbands and their wives, politicians and their followers, journalists and their listeners, authors and their readers, teachers and their students, businessmen and their clients, coaches and their players, administrators and their employees/clients, doctors and their patients, the clergy and their congregants, parents and their children, musicians and their fans, people and their divine helpers, et cetera.

The human body is a complex set of machines fixed together operating on the principles of internal and external communication. Glands communicate with target organs, heart communicates with blood vessels, lungs communicate with the airways, mouth communicates with the stomach, kidneys communicate with the urethra, testes communicate with the penis, ovaries communicate with the vagina, skin communicates with the environment, et cetera. In the cellular world, hormones released by nervous and endocrine systems accurately communicate with their effecter cells to bring desired outcome or result. Any breach in this principle of accuracy leads to several metabolic crises manifesting in the numerous medical conditions we experience and witness in our today medicine. These are the fundamental principles upon which God built the human body. Let us take a cue from the happenings in the cellular world and apply them in our physical world and we will be heading towards accomplishing our earthly and eternal task by reaching the top safely and soundly.

Show gratitude to all people who have played critical roles in your life. Wish them well on recognized notable days; birthdays, workers' days, mothers' days, fathers' day, anniversaries such as wedding, Christmas days, Easter and national events or holidays. Surprise them with gifts in the form of appreciation. Your helpers may not necessarily need these things but this gesture further strengthens your relationship with them and paints a positive picture about you to them.

---

5. HONESTY AND RELIABILITY

In the absence of truth, facts are acceptable. But as soon as fact appears before truth, it becomes nothing other than a lie. It's only the truth that will set us free. Our world is in crises today because only few people are reliable and honest. Businesses, educational institutions, churches, health facilities, the arts, et cetera are underperforming and failing because we have lost the virtue of honesty and reliability. Honesty and reliability are lost virtues for the masses but golden virtues for great achievers. To get to the top, you ought to grasp these virtues, effectively and efficiently apply them to the latter. Trust is very expensive and costly. It's hard to come by. It can't be given to cheap people. People can only trust you on the virtue of honesty and reliability.

Never for a second, think of compromising these virtues. If other people will look out for these qualities in you, your divine helpers will not be exceptions. Be a reliable and an honest person no matter what it will cost you. When your divine helpers have fully become aware of how truly reliable and honest you are to them in all matters and dealings, they will forgetfully and willingly bless you with things they wouldn't have given you if they were in their rightful state of mind. If you skilfully and tactfully deploy this powerful tool in handling people, the top will be attainable. Reliability is simply being there for people and providing all the support you can to them in moments and situations where they need your services most. Honesty is just being truthful at all material moment and time. This is not to misconstrue reliability with pleasing people at the expense of your life and happiness. You cannot do all for people but strive to help them in small ways you can.

6. HARDWORK AND FAITHFULNESS

Everyone loves a winner. People only associate themselves with winners. Achievers are winners. Winners only become winners after going through series of hard work ordeals. Hard work pays. Hardwork is a bridge that connects you to success. Until, you work hard, you merely wish to become successful. Hard work makes you accomplish tasks, fulfil your destiny, live meaningfully, influence others, command respect and regard, lovable by others, attracts and keeps your divine helpers with you. To wear the crown, you must be willing to go through the mill. No achievement is mean. You must spend sleepless nights, defy the odds, and shun the worldly pleasures in most cases before you can make recognizable impact. Another simple truth you must know is people associate themselves with hardworking people. Everyone hates lazy people. Laziness stinks and causes severe repulsion. No one blesses a lazy man. However, no one hesitates to support a hard working person so do your divine helpers.

To be faithful means to remain loyal to something or someone. Faithfulness is just remaining faithful to your goals and convictions. Serve your generation with a sense of urgency and commitment. Treat others with care and remain faithful to your dear ones especially, your divine helpers. "Winners embrace hard work. They love the discipline of it, the trade-off they're making to win. Losers, on the other hand, see it as punishment. And that's the difference" Lou Holtz observed.

PERSONAL SACRIFICE AND COMMITMENT

Personal sacrifice and commitment to one's vision, goals and plans is the simple fundamental principle and fuel that starts, drives, guides and sustains the success vehicle on the road to its desired destination. This chapter addresses few of these fundamental fuels.

DEVELOP PERSONAL PRINCIPLES AND STAY GLUED TO THEM

We are living in an extremely competitive and challenging world that is constantly trying to make us what we are not or wish to become. There are a lot of several distracters that keep altering our plans and our visions day in and day out. The systems, economic transformations, our friends, colleagues at work, family members, society, et cetera are putting forceful and almost unavoidable pressures on us to conform to what was not in our initial plans. In order to avoid or limit these pressures, you must as a matter of fact, develop personal principles and stay glued to them. These are basic life principles that put your life on track if duly adhered to. Staying glued to these principles come with personal sacrifice and commitment.

You should have absolute control over what you want to use your money to do, when you should sleep, when you should wake up, what you should eat and at what time, where to go, the profession you want, where you want to work, what programmes or gatherings you should attend, what books you should read and audio messages you should listen to, what movies or videos or television programmes you should watch and games you should watch or play. If you stick to these principles, you would clearly observe that your life pattern and rhythm will gravitate in a certain direction you have full control over. If you don't develop and maintain these basic principles, people and systems in this world will control and manipulate your life. You are doomed and your life would extinct if you allow these unfavourable worldly systems and people to control what you were created to control. Develop honesty, humility, respectfulness, hard work, competence, faithfulness, prayerful lifestyle and a thankful heart. Hold unto these values because you need them in achieving excellence in your endeavour.

IF YOU WANT TO GROW VERY TALL, WIDEN YOUR BASE

Any tall triangle I have ever seen has a very broad base. I have never seen a very tall triangle with a narrow base. The broad base supports the height of the triangle. The secret is that, if you want to grow very tall in life with so much influence and recognition, widen your base. To widen your base means to prepare yourself adequately in your field of endeavour. For your information, adequate preparation and constant training precede excellence. To widen your base means you must be very prayerful and spiritually sound for life's battle. For we wrestle not against flesh and blood but against the rulers, against the authorities and principalities, against the powers of this dark world, and against the spiritual forces of evil in the heavenly realms.

The higher you go in life, the more spiritual you should become because your enemies and evil wishers increase in number. To widen your base means you should be able to firmly cope with all the new technological and the ever-changing trends in your field of endeavour. It is technology that is ruling our world today. New trends keep coming every now and then. To stay in the game, you need technological inclination. Don't be left behind. To widen your base means to master and fully have total control over what you do by doing it exceptionally. Many people are doing what you do; so the only way to get recognized is when you do it exceptionally. To widen your base means to abreast yourself with new ways of doing things. There are several solutions to one problem. Don't stick to only one style, have other alternatives. That is what makes you unique. "When you do the common things in life in an uncommon way, you will command the attention of the world", observed George Washington Carver. To widen your base means you should have much and updated information in your field of operation. Information is power. You need more information and you should have more relevant information than your contemporaries if you want to stay ahead. To widen your base, you must be someone who researches, reads and studies a lot. Research and studies make you know more. It is the amount of knowledge you have in you that makes the difference.

To widen your base, you must periodically upgrade your academic life. Acquire valuable certificates. Engage yourself in refresher courses constantly. Try and acquire additional certificates. Attend seminars, conferences, programmes, et cetera. Your value and worth diminish when your certificates become outdated, common and ordinary. If you don't upgrade yourself, the younger ones will bypass and overtake you. You become their servant and they become your boss. Don't compete with people though. Don't envy anyone too. Just do your best and leave the rest in God's hands. Prepare to stand out and you will surely stand out. After you have systematically and strategically made all these sacrifices and commitments, your base is broadly widened to shoot and catapult you higher.

In the corporate world, if you want your business, organization, company or institution to receive an international recognition for providing quality services and products, you must employ employees who have broadened their base and be willing to pay for their expensive services. The already-broadened base employees will broaden and widen the base of your organization. The results and rewards are enormous as your business hits the lime light because of its broad base. That is what Manchester City Football Club did in 2010 when they bought world class players into the team. Just two years later, they became a top-notch club in European Champions League. Another way to achieve this is that: if you can't employ already-broadened base employees, add value to your employees who did not have broad base before joining your company. Organize frequent seminars and conferences for them. Sponsor their refresher courses or motivate them to do the courses if they can sponsor it by themselves. By doing so consistently, they will someday broaden their base and you will achieve your aim.

GOING THE EXTRA MILE

"To achieve excellence in any field of endeavour, you must go the extra mile. To go the extra mile, you must over perform. To over perform, you must over

prepare. To over prepare, you must over practice. To over practice, you must over learn. To over learn, you must provide extra effort. To provide extra effort, you need more time. But time is limited. You must therefore use time wisely. Don't spend it doing unprofitable things." - Edward Etse Aloryito

It is a personal sacrifice and commitment to take a decision to go the extra mile. This is because everyone stops on the finishing line. No one crosses the finishing line and still keeps running. To many people, it is insane to do that. Yes it is insane! I believe it and I believe you believe it too! It is paradoxical, right? Yes it is! It doesn't make sense at the first sight but with meditation and mental exercise, it makes a lot of sense and meaning. The runner is just signalling and telling you that his capacities and abilities are more than what you think. The runner is just telling you that he doesn't deserve to be in track with those who raced with him because they are not his equal. It is a sign to inform you that he deserves better treatment and consideration. It is a sign to inform you that he doesn't deserve where you placed him. His worth is more than that level. It is an indication to confirm to you that you have placed him at a wrong place and in a wrong contest. It is a typology of putting cheetah and antelope to a sprinter contest. People with these qualities are assured of excellence in any field of endeavour. It is only the insane ones who can make a meaningful difference in this life. You sometimes must appear insane to insane people. It is good but funny for a wise man to appear to foolish people foolish at the first sight. That is the irony of life.

Jesus Christ illustrated in the Holy Book the relevance and significance of extra oil or mile. The ten girls Jesus spoke about were all holy virgins but because five of these virgins failed to take extra oil with them, Jesus described them as "foolish virgins". The irony here is that as at the time the virgins took off from their homes to go and meet the bridegroom, the real foolish virgins saw the wise virgins as fools. This is because it was absurd for them to take along extra things and oil which would make their journey cumbersome and tiresome. They decided to travel light because they didn't want to suffer and dirty their clothes with oil. To them if they should carry extra oil, they were likely to dirty themselves with it and they may not look presentable and appealing to the bridegroom.

This was their mentality all this while - until the bridegroom tarried to come. When the bridegroom tarried to come, their mentality totally changed. It was then that they realized their stupidity and foolishness. It was too late for them to take any tangible action. This happens almost every day at our various work places. The wretched colleague at the workplace or student doing all the undefined works, the dirty works, comes to work or school early and leaves very late. You think he is foolish. When the time comes for God to reward his efforts, you will now realize who the real fool is.

It is obligatory to do whatever task you have been assigned to do. But it is optional to do additional tasks. It is not compulsory to do a work you weren't or haven't been assigned to do. Doing exactly what you have been asked to do, make you normal. It makes you ordinary. It means you are average. It makes you one of the lots. You therefore deserve normal treatment because you do normal things. You deserve to be called and added to the lots because you do what the lots do. Your status must remain common because you do common things. But when you do additional tasks at the work place and do them well, your treatment changes from normality to special. Your value moves from common to uncommon. Your name is mentioned with respect and honour. Your colleagues as a sign of respect give you way when you are coming. Your allowances start increasing. Your name is celebrated. These and many others are the gifts that come with going the extra mile. George Kojo Addison said, "The mile race is for average people but the extra mile race is for people with excellence." Brian Tracy noted, "If you do more than you are paid, you will always be paid more than you are doing now." You need to possess extra oil or go the extra mile so that in the event of an eventuality, you can survive.

To go the extra mile, you must over learn, over study, over research, over sell, over run, over think, over imagine, over plan, over act, over pray, over read, over train/practice, over risk and over expect. Overdo the average and normal things. Do abnormal excellent things. Excellence is not for normal things and normal people. Excellence is for the abnormal thinkers and doers. In 2007 when Sir Alex Ferguson was in charge of Manchester United FC as the manager and head coach, anytime the entire team had finished with their training session, they had to wait for Christiano Ronaldo for extra minutes. Why? Whilst every player was tired and relaxing in the bus, Christiano was still on the pitch seriously training. This continued for many months. You know what happened the following year? He became the first English Premier League Player to have won the World Best Player Award in 2008. This is strategic ways to the top. No one has equalled that record yet. Extra mile rewards. Extra mile pays.

WATCH YOUR LANGUAGE AND ATTITUDE

"You and I go through life with an awesome power – like fire or electricity or nuclear energy – right under our noses, one that can produce death or life, depending on how it is used", remarked Joyce Meyer. Your articulation is a mirror reflection of your past, present and the future. It is also a reflection of whether you are bitter or better in all situations. Just like how a farmer waters his seed with the right amount of water after sowing so that it can germinate, so it is with our tongue. The farmer doesn't stop there but he continues to water and nurture the seedling until it grows and bears fruits. In the same measure and proportion, we must continually irrigate our visions by constant declarations and decrees concerning the vision. It is a necessity and you must be able to verbalize, internalize and emotionalize your vision until it becomes part and parcel of your daily thoughts and actions.

Your future is in your mouth. Whatever you declare and decree comes to being. Whether you accept it or not, it is a divine rule. You must therefore declare positive things. How we speak, what we speak, where we speak and whom we speak to have greater consequences on our destiny. Many young professionals in various fields of practice or expertise have made shipwreck of their professional lives by the constant emission of negative words and a dilution of team morale or spirit making disparaging and derogatory remarks. Sadly, they also allow themselves for others of their kind to pour cold water on their dreams by making negative comments and gossips about others and their organizations which affects their momentum.

Your language attracts people to you or repels them from you. Beware what comes out of you because it could spell doom for you and end your career prematurely and abruptly. Before you make a speech or comment in public, you must have rehearsed your words, sieve and screen them before they come out of you. Don't allow your bad mood to dictate to you what words you should use at any material moment in your life. You can have your happy mood back just in few minutes but your words can't come back. Moods can swing or change, words don't change. How far you go in life sometimes depends on how you treat and handle people. How good or bad you handle people is determined by your way of interaction with them. The way you talk to people demonstrates how you interact with them. How do you talk to your superiors? How do you talk to your colleague workers? How do you talk to your school mates? How do you talk to elderly in the society? What kind of comments do you make about leaders of the nation? How do you talk to your teachers? How do you talk to your parents and siblings? You must be polite in speech because it pays.

Be silent when you are supposed to be working instead. Be silent if you may have to eat your words later. Be silent if you have already said it more than one time. Be silent when you are tempted to tell an outright lie. Be silent if your words will damage someone else's reputation. Be silent if your words will damage a friendship. Be silent if you would be ashamed of your words later. Be silent if your words would convey the wrong impression. Be silent if the issue is none of your business. Be silent in the heat of anger. Be silent when you don't have all the facts. Be silent when you haven't verified the story. Be silent if your words will offend a weaker person. Be silent when it is time to listen. Be silent when you are tempted to make light of holy things. Be silent when you are tempted to joke about sin. These are the only ways you can control your tongue. These are biblical and universal principles everyone must adopt in life.

The famous Nigerian preacher Pastor Chris Oyakhilome counselled, "Never use abusive and insulting language against leaders. It is wrong. When you use insulting language, it means you are of a poorer brain. It means you are of a lesser quality. The excellent minds never insult. There are higher words and levels of communication. Never repeat a scandal. You should have tumult rung for that. You should have tumult excellence for that. Train yourself to use excellent language, to speak in praise worthy terms. Use helpful and comforting words. Leave the dirty job for others. Leave it for those who are untrained, who are uncivilized. Practice high ideals. Make a difference."

Your attitude to life ultimately gives you your altitude. John Maxwell puts it, "Your attitude determines your altitude". The level of height of one's life or work is not only determined by one's skills and abilities, but also by one's manner and approach to life and work. Your attitude in simply put is your mentality, approach and manner in doing things that you do. Your educational qualification will secure you a job but it is your attitude that maintains you there. Have a positive mental attitude and that will create more miracles and opportunities for you. Have the winning attitude and mentality. Love what you do and do what you love. When talents and gifts are unmistakably identified, you will eventually love what you do and do what you love. Don't be a worker full of criticism and complaints. Don't criticize your bosses, your colleague workers, your customers, your organization or institution. These are negative attitudes. They won't take you anywhere. They will rather land you in a ditch and bring your bright future to an abrupt end. If you are very hard working but complaints a lot, people around you tend to forget all your hardwork and only remember how excessively and continuously you like complaining. All your hard work will go unnoticed and you will be tagged as a complainant. You see what a negative attitude can do to a positive attitude? Negative attitude always overshadows a positive attitude. If you don't like something change it, if you can't change it, change your perceptions and the way you think about it. Period!

If you want to go far in life, travel with likeminded people. Associate yourself with people who will bring out the best attitude in you not the worst attitude in you. Your choices of friends have an influence on your attitude. We all have positive and negative attitudes embedded in us. Your choice of friends reveals the dominant attitude that you exhibit. Choose well. Winston Churchill noted, "Attitude is a little thing that makes a big difference." In this our challenging and extremely competitive world, nothing is easy but you have to make it easy. By making it easy, you have to position yourself with the right attitude. Yoshi Kalpa remarked, "If your attitude is positive, every problem has a solution."

There are two workers; Millicent and Michelle. They are of the same grade and position. They have the same qualification. Millicent is the Unit Head in Tema whilst Michelle is the Unit Head in Koforidua. They have received a directive from their boss that they should submit their monthly report to the Head Office before the beginning of the succeeding month. Millicent submits her report to the Head Office by the close of every month whilst Michelle submits hers one week after the month has ended. There is a difference between Millicent and Michelle. The difference is that Michelle is indifferent or unresponsive to deadline. Michelle is always late in sending her report and she does not see any wrong doing with that. The difference in Millicent and Michelle is in their attitude towards work. When it comes to promotion, which of them do you think would be given the opportunity? Your guess is as good as mine.

STAY FOCUSED

There is a continuous wind blowing in this world. There is a wind that constantly blows in your opposite direction trying hard to send you to places you don't desire. Many things steal our attention. Stay focused on your goals and your dreams. Pay no attention to things trying to catch your attention. If you are not focused in life, you can't go far. Every day comes with its own troubles and challenges. There are inevitable discouraging and distraught situations that come our way almost every day. Yet you must stay strong and focused. Achievers are focused people and focused people are achievers. Anytime you turn to look at the past, you have actually started walking backwards into your future. Moving backwards into the future will end you in a ditch because you will not be able to see and jump over the necessary gutters ahead of life's journey. There are many regrettable things about the past but leave them behind you and focus on the present and the future. Today was yesterday's future.

If you want a better tomorrow or future, you must better today. If you don't better today, you can't have a better tomorrow. You can't better today if you use today thinking about yesterday's failure.

So far, I haven't regretted any major decisions I took in life. That doesn't mean I haven't failed before in life. No! I have failed many times. But to regret is to look at the past. To look at the past is to look back. To look back is to move your life in retrogression. Look forward instead of looking backward. All I know is all things work together for good. However, you must learn lessons from past failures. That is a sign of maturity. Don't allow distractions like high affinity for money, position, and popularity cloud your vision. They may be suicidal. Don't also allow career obstacles sway you off your target. Stay convicted and connected to your dreams and ensure their accomplishment. I hail from a poor family and had a lot of challenges in my financial life especially in my academic endeavours but that never made me to ever think for a second that I should compromise my education and ambitions. Don't focus on your current situations because most of them have a short gestational period.

Don't focus too much on past successes, commendations, promotions and achievements. When you focus on these things too much, you lose a firm grip of the future. Your future is more relevant than your past. There are more successes, more commendations, more promotions, and more achievements ahead of you. You have reached where you are today because of what you did in the past. If you don't do anything today to bring your achievement tomorrow, don't expect a miracle achievement tomorrow. Don't over celebrate your past achievements! Lay aside all trophies and stay focused. Some people become so arrogant with little or unrecognizable achievements. God weighs your heart before putting something in your hands. Develop and maintain the spirit of humility.

Humility brings honour. I have interacted with so many people who keep trumpeting their past achievements. Meanwhile they have no achievement to boast of today simply because they have allowed their unrecognizable past achievements to cloud their vision and eventually making them invisible in life. Don't be a victim! Stay focused! Forward ever, backwards never!

BE PREPARED TO LEAD

"Leadership is a choice you make, not a place you sit." argued, John Maxwell. If you want to stand out and be counted, then you must be prepared to lead. How do you become a leader? Note these relationships. No apprentice, no master. No student, no lecturer. No follower, no leader. No employee, no employer. You can't be a master without becoming an apprentice first; you can't be a tutor without becoming a student first; et cetera. This is a natural law that must take its course always. However, most people want to take short cut route to the top. They are slow to follow but are quick to lead. They have forgotten that the principles of leadership are better learnt whilst following other leaders. Leadership is a journey and for that reason the learning continues as long as the journey lasts. All great leaders took time to learn from their masters.

The first thing to do is to be able to successfully lead yourself. You can't lead others if you can't lead yourself. You must know your strength and weaknesses well in order to lead yourself. On the strategic ways to the top, a lot of temptations, tests and trials will come your way. Your ability to stay calm and maintain your composure in the midst of trials and temptations will prove your courage. Control your emotions even in the face extreme provocation. Don't allow money to motivate you in your leadership endeavours. If you fail in leadership, you are on the verge of ending your career in a ditch. You must be a man of action. You must always be where the action is. A leader must not shirk responsibilities. Everybody's attention is on where the action takes place. People can only notice you when you are at the action site. Be a leader with the eagle mentality and attributes. Eagles undergo a painful change of their beak and claws at age 40 when the situation demands it. This makes them strong and active again for the next 30 years or so. You must be agreeable to change when situations demand it. You must be versatile and must be able to fit in every department or field. Many young men and women are willing to get to the top yet, are failing to go to where the action is.

Go the extra mile by correctly doing things you have not been asked to do. It is a sign of been proactive. This puts you ahead of your contemporaries. Don't wait to receive instructions before you do that which you can perfectly do. At your place of work, go outside your domain and do things you are not asked to do but which remain very critical to the progress of the company or organization. Remember to play the game of life well. Play it with all fairness yet with a winning mindset. Stick to all the rules of the game. When dealing with political parties and politicians as a leader of a corporate organization, you must be very smart not to score yourself own goal by committing a professional foul. Don't belong to any camp if you want to win. You must be a problem solver. No one looks for a leader who can't solve problems. You must remain selfless and put desire for money behind you.

An eagle was sitting on a tree resting, doing nothing. A small rabbit saw the eagle and asked him, "Can I also sit like you and do nothing?" The eagle answered: "Sure, why not?" So, the rabbit sat on the ground below the eagle and rested. All of a sudden, a fox appeared, jumped on the rabbit, and ate it. The lesson we must learn here is: To be sitting doing nothing, you must be sitting very, very high up.

A turkey was chatting with a bull. "I would love to be able to get to the top of that tree," sighed the turkey, "but I haven't got the energy." "Well, why don't you nibble on some of my droppings?" replied the bull. "They're packed with nutrients." The turkey pecked at a lump of dung, and found it actually gave him enough strength to reach the lowest branch of the tree. The next day, after eating some more dung, he reached the second branch. Finally after a fourth night, the turkey was proudly perched at the top of the tree. He was promptly spotted by a farmer, who shot him out of the tree. The lesson is: Bullshit might get you to the top, but it won't keep you there.

A little bird was flying south for the winter. It was so cold; the bird froze and fell to the ground into a large field. While he was lying there, a cow came by and dropped some dung on him. As the frozen bird lay there in the pile of cow dung, he began to realize how warm he was. The dung was actually thawing him out! He lay there all warm and happy, and soon began to sing for joy. A passing cat heard the bird singing and came to investigate. Following the sound, the cat discovered the bird under the pile of cow dung, and promptly dug him out and ate him. The lessons are: Not everyone who "shits" on you is your enemy, not everyone who gets you out of shit is your friend, and when you're in deep shit, it's best to keep your mouth shut!

EFFECTIVE FINANCIAL AND PEOPLE MANAGEMENT

This is a crucial and relevant topic as far as the journey to personal growth and development, success, power and dominion is concerned. On the journey to the top, you cannot relegate or neglect the power of money. Money cannot buy life but it can prolong the life span of an individual. In this model, we would learn new ways of making, handling and growing money for our financial freedom. It is unfortunate how the church has severally demonized money. Thus it is difficult for a rich man to make heaven. But, I am sure your thoughts will be renewed after reading this shocking revelation from the Bible.

Money and possessions are the second most referenced topic in the Bible. Money is mentioned more than eight hundred (800) times. And the message is clear. Nowhere in scripture is debt viewed in a positive way. Out of the thirty-eight (38) recorded parables of Jesus Christ, sixteen (16) deal with money and possessions. In the Gospels, one out of ten verses (288 in all) deal directly with the subject of money. The Bible offers five hundred (500) verses on prayer, less than five hundred (500) on faith, but more than two thousand (2000) verses on money and possessions.

Money in itself is not evil but sometimes the desperation to make large sums of money makes people resort to immoral and criminal activities. We must not be so desperate to make large sums of money and do all kinds of evil and unacceptable things. We are the children of God. Do not struggle to make and grow money because all riches have been made available unto us. Just command it with faith and back it with the laws governing its acquisition and management.

And my God will meet all your needs according to his glorious riches in Christ Jesus. (Philippians 4:19)

There are lots of laws governing every single thing that we see with our eyes including money. But only twenty percent (20%) of the world's population knows about the laws governing the acquisition and handling of money. As you progressively flip through this great piece with rapt attention to each sentence, paragraph, and sub topic in this chapter, you will soon know the laws governing the acquisition and handling of money. These laws are universal principles. Here we go. Money making or acquisition revolves around four major pillars or steps. Know them and use them:

STEPS TO FINANCIAL FREEDOM

Everything in life involves steps and strategies. God in the creation of the universe used steps and strategies and He eventually came up with the awesome and adorable universe full of wonderful creatures. Creation was step-wise, systematic and strategic because God used different days to create different things epitomizing His systematic and strategic nature. When you follow the creation story keenly, you will realize and appreciate the architectural strategies of God. As His children, we must also exhibit His strategic prowess in every aspects of our life. In our finances, we must strategize; here we go.

EARN ALL YOU CAN

Yes, earn all you can! Earn as much money as you can! Have multiple strings of income! One or two source(s) of income is/are not enough to sustain you. How do you achieve this? The answer is simple and obvious - Your talents, gifts and skills. Please re-read the chapter on talents. Take your time and carefully identify your talents. Your talents, gifts and skills can generate for you multiple income. Your professional work should not be the only source of income. Find out what talents and gifts you have. Develop them and utilize them because that's where your wealth lies. You need money to remain in the game. You can only be in possession of money when you have multiple strings of income. Work smart and hard and use your brain more in this model. Don't chase money. Let money chase you. Improve yourself by improving and developing your talents, gifts, and skills. You will automatically be in demand because your services and products are in demand. When you are in demand; people, companies, institutions will be willing to pay any amount of money you charge. They believe in you and know your services and products are of quality. You should not freely do things for people especially when you know that your services are in great demand. Place value on yourself else people will over exploit you.

Engage your money in ventures that will bring you additional income. There are many financial opportunities around. As the famous and popular

Ghanaian motivational speaker Emmanuel Dei Tumi said sometime back that, "We are in the era of mind power not man power. Develop your mind". Use your mind to make money not your man power. If you have deep love for singing, decoration activities, writing, speaking, teaching, artistic things, drumming, instruments, research, playing with children and keeping them happy, et cetera, you can make huge incomes from these things aside your professional work. How do you do this? For instance, if you can teach, gather children in your hood and start teaching them. After three or five meetings with them, their parents would realize improvement in their wards academic performance. The parents will now want your services as a part time teacher for their wards because they have realized how beneficial you can be to their children. In this case, you charge them. This magic works whether you are a professional teacher or not. It has worked for me. It will work for you too. Why don't you charge for your drumming or singing or decorative skills? You have no idea how many women who want young people to play with their children whilst they (women) can attend to other pressing needs. They are willing to pay for such services. Find out!

SAVE ALL YOU CAN

As you earn money from multiple sources, your savings increases. You must develop and maintain the habit of savings. No matter how little money you earn as an income, you must try by all means to save a little percentage of it. Savings is a sign of mental maturity. Achievers are mentally matured people and mentally matured people are achievers. You can't successfully reach the top if you lack the diligence and discipline to cultivate the habit of savings. Savings projects you and gives you hope for the future. Spend your surplus after you have saved what you really wanted to save. Don't be an impulse buyer. Don't buy things on impulse. About 90% of the things we buy on impulse are things we don't need.

Meanwhile impulse buying is one of the greatest challenges hindering our ability to save. Impulse buyers are people who can't save any money at all. If it is not part of your monthly or weekly or daily budget, then you don't need it. It is a known fact that if you buy things you do not need, soon you will have to sell things you need.

Prepare monthly, weekly and daily financial budgets and be guided by it. Be diligent and discipline enough to stick to your budget. If you are not ready to prepare budget for your expenditure, then you are not ready for the success journey to the top. Cut down unnecessary spending. Don't always carry too much money on you. It is very tempting. Your budget should always be less than your income so that you can save the difference for future purposes. Avoid debts and borrowing. When you are in possession of money at any material moment, control and restrict your appetite. Try to avoid drinking and smoking. Save the money you will use to engage in such activities. Drinking and smoking will even compound your health problems and make you spend more money seeking medical care. Avoid trying to financially impress friends in public places or gatherings. Save those monies rather because you need them in the future. Save with any reliable banking institution, "susu" companies, cooperatives, credit unions, money boxes, et cetera. It is true that empty pockets teach you a million things in life but full pockets spoil you in a million ways. Beware!

INVEST ALL YOU CAN

In order to grow your business well, you must learn to hide and flourish like the snake. ***"I am sending you out like sheep among wolves. Therefore, be as shrewd as snakes and as innocent as doves", Matthew 10:16.*** One fact about snakes is that, they search for a convenient environment, hide in that place, and then, stay in those places where you least expected them to be, and flourish for their entire life. These places are mostly strange places where you would least expect snakes. A snake can find a comfortable place and hide, and then, stay in your living room with you for years without your notice. That is smartness. Learn this smartness from the snake. Be financially smart so you can hide and flourish in businesses where people least expect it.

Invest your money in reliable financial institutions. Do not just invest in one or two companies. **Don't put all eggs in one basket.** Invest in as many companies as possible. In some cases, it might appear too risky to invest in some companies or groups, be smart and don't venture. You must once again put your brain to work and let your brain guide you. Don't be consumed by the huge unrealistic returns promise. If you are not fully convinced, don't venture. **Never test the depth of a river with both feet. Honesty is a very expensive virtue. Don't expect it from cheap people. We used pencil as children but not when we became adults. As adults, our writing stick is pen. Mistakes in childhood can be erased but not now. For this reason, read and write carefully otherwise life will be a tissue paper.** There are serious business companies who are willing to give you the best offer and keep your money safe for you. Search for them and do profitable business with them. Start now!

GIVE ALL YOU CAN

Yes! Give all you can. This principle doesn't make sense to money conscious people but trust me this is the best biblical and universal principle on how to make more money. Money naturally flows towards you as you practice this principle. Don't forget this. Give with an open and pure heart. Give with a good motive else your giving will be in vain. "Give and it will be given to you. A good measure, pressed down, shaken together and running over, will be poured into your lap. For with the measure you use, it will be measured to you" from Luke 6:38. Be kind to people who need your support in ways you can afford. This sub-topic is explicitly digested in chapter thirteen. Don't forget to give all you can!

THE BUFFALO HUNTER

There is a story told about a professional hunter who had a friend who always wanted to go with him on one of his hunts. So one day he said to his friend, "I have a permit to go into the Zambezi Valley and hunt for a buffalo. Would you like to come with me?" The friend was happy at the opportunity. "When do we go?" he asked. "In about six months' time, but before then I have to train you about hunting expeditions."

For the next six months, the two men met every day, and they discussed and planned for the trip. The hunter's friend was surprised by how careful the hunter was about everything. He taught him about the bush, and how to survive in it. He taught him everything about buffaloes. "You must respect the buffalo," he said, "because it's a very intelligent animal, and it is also extremely dangerous."

He gave him lots of books to read, about hunting and buffaloes. During that time, the friend also trained every day at the shooting range. He understood by then the different types of guns used to hunt buffalo. He also had to do fitness training, which surprised him. "You can die out there if you are not fit," his friend explained. He was totally astonished by what he was learning about hunting". Until now, I thought all you do is just go out and shoot, but now I know there's more to this than meets the eye!" he exclaimed.

When the day came, the two men set out into the wild bush of the Zambezi Valley, one of the most beautiful places on the earth. It is also inhospitably hot, and the terrain is tough.

They'd been tracking one single animal for five (5) days, and the hunter's friend was totally exhausted. He watched as his friend patiently made careful plans every single day. The hunter seemed to take forever, from the point of view of his friend. Sometimes they would walk, and sometimes they would sit for hours. The hunter was always looking around, scanning the bushes, not even (it appeared) always paying attention to the surrounding areas more than the buffalo.

"Why can't he just shoot and we go home?" He was getting tired of this, as they walked almost fifty (50) miles a day. He was also hungry most of the time, as they only ate rations of dried meat and fruit, most of the time. The hunter looked at the animal through his gun sight over and over every day, but wouldn't take a shot. Sometimes they appeared so close, but he still did not do anything. It was the fifth day: the animal was in sight again, but the hunter was going through his routine again. The friend sat in the bushes, when suddenly a rabbit appeared in front of him and he thought to himself, "At least if I shoot this rabbit, we can have meat tonight. I'm tired of dry rations." So he pulled out his gun and fired once.

The rabbit disappeared, as he had missed anyway, but so did the buffalo, and with it, the entire herd. The hunter looked at him in total horror and disbelief! Then he shouted, "Run, or you die!" as he took off. They almost got stampeded by an entire herd that seemed to appear from nowhere. Also, suddenly there were lions everywhere that he had not seen before! But for the skills of the hunter, who led them both to safety, they could have died. The buffalo was gone. The hunt was over. They had to return home, empty-handed.

There are **at least five practical business and people management lessons** we can learn from the story above. It will serve as a case study for us as we explore the chapter.

THE BUSINESS MANAGEMENT LESSONS

1. You need thorough planning; scanning of business environment, study the opponent or target. Know when to strike (a deal), and finally make sure when you make a shot, it's the right shot or else you will go home empty handed. In business, you would have lost blatantly.

2. Don't be impatient, pay attention, have a desire or passion for that particular business. Read books about your subject matter. Respect your field or business. Learn survival tactics. Vigorously train yourself on regular basis. Attend seminars and be willing to be taught. Strategize and understand or know the business principles. Listen to words of wisdom.

3. The "friend" here could be a member of your team, or staff. You must choose people who not only understand that you are on a buffalo hunt, but also what it takes to secure the prize. More often than not, you will find out that whilst people will understand the vision when you start off, once the going gets tough, they replace that vision with their own narrow vision of the rabbit hunt. These are the people who start to moan and question your strategy behind the scenes. It takes great leadership to keep everyone in the buffalo hunt.

4. Whatever you are trying to do in business, you must always be acutely aware that there are competitors out there; these are the "lions" of our story. The experienced hunter knew they were there. He had to choose a moment when he could get the job done in such a way, that he would not have simply

fed some hungry lions. This is what is called "the wisdom of the hunt"; it's much more than an issue of timing.

5. Don't forget the herd: The hunter was interested in a particular animal, and not just any buffalo in the herd. He never lost sight of that particular animal, once he had selected it. He also understood at all times that the greatest protection of a buffalo comes from the herd (the other Buffaloes). The "herd" could be the environment, or the regulators, and all those who want to protect the status quo. These are those forces that the buffalo can call on for protection. The experienced hunter knew that the "herd" was there and had to be navigated. If it was spooked, the unintended consequences could be disastrous. Every major new business initiative has to face the "herd" at some time: Uber is at war with taxi operators around the world. Google faces regulators in Europe.

6. The mission was not only to kill a buffalo, but to bring it back home with them. Bringing it back is the toughest part of the mission. Sometimes ending the task in business contracts successfully is the most difficult hurdle to cross.

7. Never allow small things to distract you from the big trophy. Stay focused.

LESSONS ON PEOPLE MANAGEMENT

- Train your partners or followers on regular basis and teach them survival tactics.

- Add value to their lives by allowing them to attend seminars and conferences.
- Let your partners or employees or followers understand all the principles in human management.
- Always let your partner(s), staff or subjects know why you have not taken a shot yet even when it appears, timely to shoot.
- Leave no partner or staff in the dark especially when you are taking the lead.

TIME IS LIMITED; FORGET NOT THY ROOT AND KNOW WHERE THOU GOETH

Time is life. Time is money. Time is opportunity. Time is strength. Time is success. Time is victory. In fact, time is everything. However, time is very limited especially if you don't maximize it. It is limited because we don't have all the time. God is so wise that He has given each one of us equal amount of time in a day. This implies that He has given each one of us an equal opportunity on daily basis. What you use each day for determines where you will reach in future and how your life will be.

Those who have judiciously utilized their time are the difference makers and the top notch people in our society. Effective time management brings fulfillment and prevents disgrace.

What do you use your time for? What time do you wake up in the morning? How many minutes or hours do you use in getting ready for school or work? How many tasks do you successfully accomplish in a day? Do you have daily tasks schedule nicely written on paper and folded into your pocket before leaving home? What do you use your leisure time for? How many minutes or hours do you use to develop your talents, gifts and skills on daily basis? How many minutes or hours do you spend in doing things that add no value to your life? How many things you could have done in the day but you pushed them into the future because you don't feel like performing them? How many minutes or hours do you spend with your Maker in a day? What time do you retire to bed at night? How do you spend your weekend? After honestly answering these questions, you will know where you belong.

Let's do some small arithmetic here. Be truthful and honest with yourself. Just take a pen and paper and calculate the number of minutes or hours you spend in a day doing unprofitable things. Multiply that number by seven. That will total the number of hours you have wasted in a week. Continue further and multiply your final value by fifty-two. You will get an amazingly huge number. That is the number of hours you have willingly and happily wasted in one year. Imagine your age mate and a colleague worker or student judiciously utilized that time that you have wasted; is he or she not ahead of you in life? If you spend only 30 minutes in a day doing unprofitable things, you will be wasting 10,920 minutes (182 hours) in one year. You will be wasting a whopping 910 hours in five years. Pause and just imagine how much time you have wasted in the past years. The unhealthy conversations, movies, games, plays, et cetera.

On the journey to the top, there is no time to waste. Never compromise your sleep either. That will deteriorate your health and give you complications. Just make good and effective use of the hours in the day.

Do your best to accomplish daily schedule tasks. Stick to your plans and act them out. Make sure you read materials that will develop your talents every day. The most powerful and strongest tool you have in this world is your talent. Develop it daily. You can only become a star when you develop your talent on daily basis. Do not allow unnecessary things to steal your attention. Discipline yourself and try as much as possible not to allow friends control your movements and influence you with their plans for the day. Don't be a slave to the dictates of your friends. They have no idea where God wants to send you. Manage your time! It is keen in your progress. They are the very people who will make derogatory remarks about you when you fail in your endeavours. Pray to God and commit every daily plan into His hands for divine and perfect direction.

Remember this. You have well written and calculated visions, goals, and objectives you want to accomplish. These can only be realized when you make daily commitment by acting your plans and strategies. Start making that commitment now and your vision will be actualized.

WHAT WILL BE YOUR LAST WISH?

On his death bed, Alexander the Great summoned his army generals and told them his three ultimate wishes:

- The best doctors should carry his coffin.
- The wealth he has accumulated (money, gold, precious stones) should be scattered along the procession to the cemetery.
- His hands should be let loose, so they hang outside the coffin for all to see.

All his army generals were surprised by these unusual requests and one of them asked Alexander to explain. Here is what Alexander the Great had to say:

- "I want the best doctors to carry my coffin to demonstrate that in the face of death; even the best doctors in the world have no power to heal".
- "I want the road to be covered with my treasure so that everybody sees that material wealth acquired on earth, will stay on earth."
- "I want my hands to swing in the wind, so that people understand that we come to this world empty handed and we leave this world empty handed after the most precious treasure of all is exhausted, and that is: TIME."

We must learn great lessons from this. We do not take to our grave any material wealth. Time is our most precious treasure because it is limited. We can produce more wealth, but we cannot produce more time. When we give someone our time, we actually give a portion of our life that we will never take back.

Your wealth cannot buy you life even though it may prolong your earthly stay. Live a pleasing life because time is limited.

GENEROSITY AND COMMITMENT TO GOD'S WORK

One day, a newspaper reporter interviewed a farmer who grew award-winning corn each year. It was revealed that the farmer shared his seed corn with his neighbours. Confused and disturbed, the reporter asked, "How can you afford to share your best seed corn with your neighbours when they are entering their corn in competition with yours each year?" The farmer smiled knowingly and explained, "The wind picks up pollen from the ripening corn and swirls it from field to field. If my neighbours grow inferior corn, cross-pollination will gradually degrade the quality of my corn. If I am to grow good corn, I must help my neighbours grow good corn."

So it is with our lives. Those who want to live meaningfully and well must help better the lives of others. For a life to be valued, it is measured by the lives it touches. And those who choose to be happy must help others find happiness, for the welfare of each is bound up with the welfare of all. Call it power of collectivity. Call it a principle of success. Call it a law of life. The fact remains, "None of us truly wins, until we all win." In life, when you help the people around you to be good, you surely become the best. Always bear in mind that real happiness is in helping others.

Always work for a cause; not for applause. Live your life to express; not to impress. Do not strive to make your presence noticed; just make your absence felt. Nothing in nature lives for itself. Rivers do not drink their own water; trees do not eat their own fruits. The sun and the moon do not shine for themselves; and flowers do not spread their fragrance for themselves. Our teeth do not beautify our mouth for themselves. Twenty seven years of imprisonment, maltreatment and torture of Nelson Mandela was not for his own liberation and freedom. Jesus Christ did not sacrifice for Himself.

Living for others is a rule of nature. We were all born to help each other. No matter how difficult the situation you find yourself in; still do well to help others. Strive within your means to help people no matter the matter. Fact is, there will be no perfect time in your life when you will be able to satisfy all your demands. If you want to wait for the right time to come before you help others, it won't just come because our human flesh is not always satisfied with our possessions at any material moment in time. Our body is naturally selfish and craves for more. Absolutely nothing satisfies our body. You must however, be able to bring your flesh under subjection and control. You should be able to make time for people who need your services in crucial moment no matter how busy your schedules appear to be.

The greatest mistake any man can make is to lean on his own understanding and strength. Keep trusting the Lord. (Proverbs 3: 5). Support the work of God in all ways possible. If you are not a Pastor, or a church elder, or church executive, or a member of any vibrant group in the church, or working in the premises of the church or place of worship, that doesn't mean God doesn't need your services. He may need your services more than even those preaching and teaching His word or working in the church. God has blessed you because He wants you to bless His work. You can bless His work with your money and all your movable or fixed assets you have. If you can't always be present in the house of God due to one reason or another, your valuable substances He has blessed you with should also not be absent! At all! It should not happen! The whole duty of man is summarized by King Solomon in the Book of Ecclesiastes 12:13, "Now has been heard; here is the conclusion of the matter: Fear God and keep His commandment, for this is the duty of all mankind". One of the divine duties of mankind is to worship God with the substances He has blessed us with. We can't be good worshippers of God if we remain stingy in His house. Support ALL church activities with your intelligence, might, money, movable and fixed assets. ALL church activities are all. You must do and give your BEST when it comes to the work of God because He is a God of BEST.

Those who are church leaders, executives, all department leaders and members and workers in the church premises you have no grounds to disappoint God. Give God all the best you have because He deserves your best. Some people think because they are always in the house of God or are doing something in the house of God, He is pleased with them. You may be deceiving yourself. If you are not giving Him your best why should He be pleased with you? "This is my beloved Son; whom I love; in him I am well pleased" Matthew 3:17. Be committed to every church activity and do it with passion: church arrangement, decoration, evangelism, prayers, choir, et cetera. If you don't do anything for God at the church premises or in the church, you better find one or two to do. It will help and save you in so many ways. It sounds funny to me when some people think that they are so special to do certain things in the church because they immaturely think their class is higher than such duties. It is only babes who think and behave that way. Don't be one! Let God be pleased with your services to Him and mankind because that is the whole reason for your existence.

Support the less privilege people in your locality in ways you can: the orphans, widows, disabled, the aged, brilliant but needy students, single parents. Most of these people only need encouragement and motivation to bring out the best in them. Encourage and motivate them. Advise them. Communicate with them using higher ways and words of communication. Praise them. Use comforting words. Respect their views. Provide a shoulder for them to cry on when the need be. Give them your attention. Let them know that you are there for them and they are there for you. This is not to say they should entirely depend on you. Be smart to read in-between the lines. However, you can accept their entire dependency if you have the means to sustain them. Establish and maintain a strong rapport with them. That is all they need. Use this opportunity to bring out the best in them by identifying their potentials and encouraging and motivating them to better it and rise up to the challenge. Don't exploit them. That is mean. Genuinely assist them.

Provide financial assistance if you are in the capacity to do so to support those who need it most in their academic and vocational endeavours. You may not have plenty money, but let your budget cover some of these things. Play a philanthropic role. It is a seed you are sowing which you will reap in time and eternity. It is not mandatory to do this but it is honourable to do it. Remain an honourable person by practicing these high ideals. Let people be happy especially the vulnerable ones because your mother gave birth to you. Let people mention your name with honour and respect. These people always pray for you. And do you know what their prayers can do for you? Maybe you have no idea!

Use your wisdom and intelligence to teach others. Let people benefit from it. Right from the first semester to the last semester of my stay as a university student, I have spent most of my time teaching students and trying as much as possible to let them understand most difficult subjects and concepts. It isn't that I had enough time and didn't know what to use my time for that is why I was teaching students. No, far from that. It is because I was willing to go the extra mile to give the best to people who needed my services most. My colleagues will attest to the fact that I was engaged in other extra-curricular activities as well. My schedules were so tight that sometimes I went to write examination papers I was not fully prepared for. That is how far I went and risked my academic life because I wanted others to also pass their exams. In my quest to give them my best, I started analyzing students' results in order to know the subjects that are of concern to students and demand my attention (because I always wanted to teach them the most difficult subjects), I researched and learned a lot, I started writing to further develop my scope of understanding and grasping. Out of this selfless service to people, two great things have emerged: my first organization; Eminence Analytic and Research Institute, Ghana (EARIG) and my Authorship. Until you develop the habit of selflessly helping and assisting others, you will never know all your talents and develop your full potentials.

Any gift at all God has given you, use it to bless others. It is the people around you who need your talents and gifts most not you yourself. Bless people with your skills and abilities. Selfishness kills. It kills people around you and finally kills you too.

Read and recite this poem for your reading pleasure. Let this poem talk to your innermost being.

ELECTRIFY YOUR ELECTRICAL CIRCUITS

A life without addition or multiplication
Is a life of stagnation or reduction
Add value to your life in any way possible
Multiply your life in any way available
Multiply your skills in any way imaginable
Multiply your gifts in any way reliable
Because stagnation brings frustration
Whilst reduction brings confusion
Life is meaningful when it multiplies
Life is successful when it electrifies
Others in your electrical circuit
Impact is made when your circuit
Electrifies other electrical circuits
With God on our side, our circuits
Will electrify other electrical circuits

BEWARE OF THE AFRICAN SYSTEMS

On Saturday, 27th February 2016, Pastor Dr. Mensa Otabil; Founder of the International Central Gospel Church and Central University College infected and triggered a mass of young entrepreneurs with a mark performance, a destiny changing motivational message that will linger in the minds of many, for many years to come. He is loved by many, hated by some but few will deny the power of his word. It is contagious!

He was to give a major address at Albert Ocran's springboard convocation programme, but he did far more than expected. His message is worth sharing in this life transforming book. He planted, watered and nurtured a seed of holy anger in the army of entrepreneurs, hoping that anger will eventually germinate into fruits that will reverse the backwardly suffocating systems, laws and policies in Ghana; systems that served only to frustrate and kill as many dreams and businesses as possible.

THE PARABLE OF ONION AND TRAVOLATOR

He used the parable of onion and a travolator to tell the wonderful but annoying story of why Mark Zuckerberg, a 31 year old computer programmer, is richer than him (Otabil), his wife; richer than President Mahama and the MPs and richer than all Ghanaians combined. Otabil feels angry and insulted by the development because Zuckerberg, he reckoned, is not any more intelligent than the thousands of computer programmers in Ghana but the American has a better environment; a country of opportunities.

"What is the difference between Zuckerberg and you; Steve Jobs and you? Otabil asked rhetorically. "It is not brains, it is the environment," he answered angrily.

WHERE IS OUR TRAVOLATOR AND SULPHUR-FREE ONION?

The famous preacher told a story of how he travelled out of the country and with the aid of a travolator he beat a young man to a walking contest. The man decided to speed walk but he used a travolator at some point. Even though the man heeled-and-toed with swiftness, he could not beat Otabil because the travolator pushed him faster to his destination.

He told another story, he read in a book, of a US company seeking to grow onions that will not sting the eyes. For a man who had shed onion-stinging- tears in the past from his kitchen in Accra, he will certainly wonder how an American company will grow new species of onions without its notorious characteristic. But the 'useless' book he was reading in the plane suddenly became useful, revealing, that the new species of onions will be planted in a "non-sulphuric ground."

He learnt a new thing. Onions sting eyes because they are always grown and nurtured in a soil full of sulphur but the US Company is coming with a new offer. "The reason why the onions will not sting people's eyes is because it was going to be grown in sulphur free soil." It is not the nature of onions to sting eyes. It is the environment it is nurtured in that makes it sting eyes.

"It struck me that a person can be so good but if he is planted in a wrong environment, he is going to turn up so bad," Otabil said. He wondered how much sulphur was in the Ghanaian environment that made many dreams, business break down in tears. "What have we put in the environment, in the soil that is killing the dream of young men and young women? How can people go to university and for years and not know what to do? How can people with potential not fulfil their potential?"

"If you take a simple area like football, the greatest Ghanaian players now were all onions that were planted in a different soil. They had to go outside Ghana for their talents to become world class. Do you think if Michael Essien had continued playing in the Ghana league we will call his name? No! Is he talented? Yes. No matter how big the dream is, Otabil says if the environment is without a travolator or a sulphur free soil, you will achieve something but ultimately you will become the village champion amongst global players. "The challenge for nations like Ghana is not the challenge of talented citizens. It is the challenge of poisonous environment. It is an environment that has been poisoned by ordinariness, by mediocrity and sometimes by a clear agenda to destroy talents."

"And how can a nation be great when its systems are fighting the talents of its people?" he asked. It is good to dream because dream is free but fight to get a better environment for the dream to thrive; he challenged the young men and women. "We have to force the politicians to start thinking of us; of our lives; our future and dreams. And the only way to do that is for you to start thinking not in party terms but in policy terms," "Because if that doesn't happen dreamers will die with their dreams not realized," he added. What is your dream; fight for a better travolator and a sulphuric free soil, to make your dreams come to pass.

Africa is full of dream killers. Beware and study the environment and the people very well before making your dreams public. Laugh with many, never trust any. Don't share your dreams with anyone you meet around. It is not all that glitters, is gold.

DON'T EVER QUIT; GREAT LEADERS NEVER QUIT

Born into poverty, Abraham Lincoln was faced with defeat throughout his life. He lost eight elections, twice failed in business and suffered a nervous breakdown. He could have quitted many times – but he didn't and because he didn't quit, he became one of the greatest Presidents in the United States history.

Aspire to be the next Abraham Lincoln in our generation but with your own identity. Strive to create a memorable worldwide identity for yourself. Let your passion to lead others be your driving force and you will do exploits.

Dr. Kwame Nkrumah and Nelson Mandela spent years in prison with untold hardship and maltreatment yet that never made them to quit.

Professor John Evans Atta Mills never quitted contesting the presidential seat until he became the President of Ghana. Nana Addo Dankwa Akufo-Addo is still contesting the presidential seat because he belongs to these icons of excellence. Baba Jamal contested for parliamentary seat four times in the Akwatia constituency and lost all. But he finally won the fifth contest and is now a Member of Parliament in Ghana. Sarkodie recalled, "I played many shows for many show organizers and they always paid me with t-shirts and toffees, I nearly stopped raping" But because he didn't quit, he is now a living legend in the music industry. Asamoah Gyan had this to share, "My first coach once told me, you can't be a player, is better to be a ball boy for my team or just try to be a musician' I felt very bad that very moment" If Gyan had stopped, he would not have gotten the international recognition as the African Player with the highest number of goals at the World Cup Tournaments. He wouldn't have gotten all the accolades he has gotten from his football career.

During my basic school days, I had to ride bicycle to cover over seven miles before going to school. There were countless number of times when my bicycle got spoilt just at the start or in the middle of the journey to school and I had to carry it and walk to school. Sometimes I got to school as late as 11:00am. But, I never stopped schooling. Meanwhile most of my friends who walked only one mile to school quitted school because their excuse was that they can't keep walking to school every day. If I didn't quit in those times, do you think I will quit now? If I had stopped, you wouldn't have been reading this masterpiece as my product. Don't ever quit because you are a great personality!!!

Read and recite this poem for your reading pleasure. Let it rejuvenate your innermost being.

THE TOP IS REACHABLE

The top we spot from afar is reachable
The top we aspire to be is attainable
Though it is high above mediocrity
It is far below excellence mentality
It's for pursuers of excellence
It's for those with perseverance
The top remains very convenient
For those who dare to be different
For the optimistic; and not the pessimistic
For the eagles; and not chickens
The top remains good and spacious
For those who are bold or audacious
For those with visions and are able to
Convert their visions into goals
For the goals planners and plan actors
And for those who know life's purpose
We have an unfailing Source
Where we receive our resources
No matter the struggles
No matter the troubles
We'll not retreat or move backward
Because we understand life forward
His grace is sufficient
To take us to the very top

EMINENCE ANALYTIC AND RESEARCH INSTITUTE, GHANA (EARIG)

Eminence Analytic and Research Institute, Ghana (EARIG) is a national policy think tank that focuses on performance and policy analysis of educational, health, political, and economic institutions and provide appropriate guidance with expert advice and recommendations.

The institute's mission is to liberate mankind and solve problems of society through analytic thinking. Our vision is to make the world a better place to live in with minimal stress.

The three core services the institute offers are as follow:

- Analyze performance, policies and operations of the four (4) sectorial institutions: educational, health, political and economic institutions.
- Give goal-oriented expert advice on performance and policies to these sectorial institutions
- Give goal-oriented expert advice or plan and organize events for these institutions.

PROFESSIONALISM & EXCELLENCE

Request for information or enquiries or our services should be addressed to:

Postal Address:

Box BT 288, Tema, Ghana
Email: earig@gmail.com, and edwardetse@gmail.com
Website: www.earinstitutegh.com
Tel: (+233) 0245194693, 0202659394

EMINENCE INNOVATIONS

Eminence Innovations is a leadership group with the sole responsibility to inspire and empower the youth for divine destiny discovery and fulfilment. We collaborate with student groups to organize leadership and youth empowerment seminars and programs in tertiary and second cycle institutions and junior high schools. We also collaborate with religious bodies and other social groups to organize seminars that aim at empowering and challenging lives for divine peak performance.

Our mission is imparting our world with God-given mandate. Our vision is to inspire and empower transgenerational impact makers.

Request for information or enquiries or our services should be addressed to:

Postal Address:

Box BT 288, Tema, Ghana

Email: edwardetse@gmail.com

Tel: (+233) 0245194693, 0202659394

REFERENCES

Melchizedeck, A. O. (2014). The Eagle's Mindset, ISBN 978-9-9881-9048-4

Harris, H. (2004). The 12 Universal Laws of SuccesS, ISBN 987-09748-3621-8

Tinagyei S. (2013). Smart Money, ISBN 978-9-9881-9105-4

Addison G. K. (2012). Standing Out, ISBN 978-9988-1-6687-8

Enenche. P. (Video). Facts of Life

Mason J. (2004). Believe You Can, p. 72

http://science.jrank.org/pages/6118/sharks-reproductive-growth

www.ingramcontent.com/pod-product-compliance
Lightning Source LLC
La Vergne TN
LVHW010558160826
845677LV00013B/3169

* 9 7 8 9 9 8 8 2 4 1 1 0 0 *